To Kate, Quinn, Lukas, and Devin. You make me want to make the world a little bit better.

Special thanks to Dr. Rachael Pelletti for helping me edit and organize these ideas. I got in over my skis, and you helped me stay balanced.

Lifting the Lockdown:
Embracing the Evidence to Build Holistically Safe Schools

Copyright © 2025 by Jordan Werme

All rights reserved.
No part of this book may be reproduced, scanned, or distributed in any printed or electronic form without permission.

First Edition: 2025
Printed in the United States of America
ISBN: 979-8-89965-478-7

Chapter	Title	Page
	Preface	6
	Part I: Beyond Lockdown	
1	Defining School Violence	11
2	Root Causes and Contributing Factors	22
3	Cultivating Comprehensive Safety for Thriving Schools	33
4	The NRA's Role in Promoting School Violence	40
5	The Complexities of Armed Security	58
6	Case Studies from Major School Shootings	70
7	Active Shooter Drills and Well-Being	88
8	Legislation for Comprehensive Safety	92
9	Foundations of a Safe and Supportive School	98
10	The Role of School Staff in Everyday Safety	103
	Part II: A Holistic Shift	
11	Pillars of Holistic School Safety in Action	109
12	Repairing Harm and Building Community	117
13	Strong Partnerships, Safe Schools	125
14	Amplifying Student Voices for Safer Schools	132
15	Cultivating Positive School Climates	136
16	Social and Emotional Learning	140
17	Restorative Practices	148
18	Comprehensive School Mental Health	158
19	Protective Factors and Advocacy	165
20	Crisis Prevention and Intervention	175

21	The Role of Technology in Safety	182
22	Community Support for School Safety	186
23	Behavioral Health-Centered School Safety	189
24	A Culture of Safety and Well-Being	192
25	Sustainable Financial Strategies	194
26	Holistic School Safety in Your Community	203

Part III: Protection Through Connection

27	The Converging Crises	213
28	The Protective Power of Mentoring	217
29	Personal and Professional Growth	223
30	Mentoring Offers Alternatives	228
31	Isolation and a Mental Health Crises	234
32	Effective Mentoring Programs	239
33	Sustaining Mentoring Initiatives	247
34	Mentoring a More Resilient Generation	250

Postscript — 253

Appendices

Appendix A: Glossary — 257

Appendix B: Directory of Resources — 261

Work Cited — 264

Lifting the Lockdown: Embracing the Evidence to Build Holistically Safe Schools

Preface

2012 was a formative year in how I think about guns and gun violence, and in how I see United States government as complicit in the unconscionable increase of mass school shootings over the last 40-plus years.

When that year opened, I had only recently returned from my first overseas deployment, a peacekeeping mission to Kosovo, where I always carried a firearm with me. I have never owned a personal firearm, but when I joined the Army National Guard in 2002, I learned to competently use several of them – the M16 rifle and the M9 pistol, primarily. Though I was able to meet my qualification scores, firearms were never something I enjoyed using or spent extra time learning.

While in Kosovo, I was never called upon to draw or fire a weapon. My military career, while long, was not one of combat or physical conflict. I began as a journalist and photographer and finished my career without ever leaving the field of public affairs. Yet, I did leave with a working knowledge of firearms, and more importantly, a better understanding of the culture that exists around guns, gun ownership, and the potential of violence associated with it.

My wife and I started 2012 expecting twin babies in the first part of the year, and our first child had just turned two years old. All this to say that when three separate mass shootings occurred in February of 2012 (in Georgia, Tennessee, and Ohio, respectively), I was primed to take notice of these incidents in a way I hadn't before. The twins came along a few weeks early, as twins tend to do, before the end of March. A few days later, while one of my newborn baby boys was in the Neonatal Intensive Care Unit, another shooting occurred, this time in Florida.

Eventually, all five of us made it home as a family in early April, while additional shooting sprees in California and Oklahoma prevented other families from reuniting. But we were busy with a toddler and twins, changing more than 30 diapers each day and getting far too familiar with The Wiggles and Team Umizoomi to pay much attention to the news.

I've been a lifelong fan of the Batman character, and in July I lined up with millions of others across the country to see the final entry in Christopher Nolan's excellent *Dark Knight* trilogy of films, *The Dark Knight Rises* (*TDKR*). I was watching *TDKR* in Connecticut at the same time moviegoers in Aurora, Colorado were gunned down during a screening of the same film. While Bane had successfully taken the city of Gotham hostage in Nolan's universe, it seemed that unbridled gun violence was doing the same in this one. But here, we didn't have Batman to save us.

Less than a week later, my family received the devastating news that one of the twins was in liver failure, and our lives were upended. We are fortunate that all three of our kids are still with us and are generally thriving as teenagers today. I will skip the details of that period – that's not what this book is about. I bring it up because living in the Neonatal Intensive Care Unit (NICU) with your spouse and twin infants while awaiting surgeries is intense, terrifying, lifechanging, and boring.

During the long hours of sitting and waiting, I began to really read about gun violence for the first time. I learned about the history of the National Rifle Association and its unchecked influence on national legislation. I learned about mental health challenges and Constitutional issues around access to guns, and I learned about the fascinating biology of the human liver. Though none of these topics were of more than passing interest to me before 2012, they are deeply ingrained in my thinking today.

I have no aptitude, however, for medicine or biology, and so my tendency toward history, anthropology, and sociology led me to keep trying to understand the issues around gun violence, school shootings, and why – of all the countries on Earth – the United States is singularly incapable of providing any reasonable assurance of safety from violent rampages.

In December of 2012, just days after my oldest child's third birthday, the shooting at Sandy Hook Elementary School in Newtown, CT, shook the fabric of the community in a way that rivalled 9/11. For a moment there, it looked like we may have been able to pass legislation to stem the scourge of gun violence in America. But that moment passed, unrealized, and now guns account (as accidental injury, homicide, and suicide) for more juvenile deaths in America than any other factor.

When the probability of armed security in my kids' schools came up in 2019, I immediately thought back on everything I'd learned and wondered why this was the go-to measure. I'd seen the evidence, read the statistics, followed the news reports, and had access to all the same publicly available information as anyone else had. Why do 80 percent of American adults support increasing the presence of firearms in schools when the data (and the federal government) firmly conclude that these measures are ineffective, and even counterproductive and more destructive than taking no action at all?

I've since made multiple public addresses, written multiple short papers, and had many conversations with local policymakers on this topic. What I've learned is that, generally speaking, until the public demands an alternate approach, most people in a position to enact change in positive directions will be unwilling to do so.

My hope is that the history, data, and perspectives shared in this book will help drive conversation and change in the public narrative around what makes schools safer. We can't just put a gun in a school and expect that school to be a safer place; we must make long-term investments in multifaceted areas of our communities to cultivate positive climates in schools and the wider population.

This book includes context and data, as well as immediate actions each us can take to bring awareness of real best practices that prevent violence. Through these collective efforts we can create a holistic environment for learning, growth, creativity, and safety for our kids.

Jordan Werme
June 2025

Part I:
Beyond Lockdown

Chapter 1: Defining School Violence

My personal views on the primary means by which most districts attempt to patch together a school safety plan have left me labelled as anti-police or soft on the issue. In reality, I am not against the concepts of law enforcement, crime prevention, or the presence of security professionals in schools. However, when I think about "school security," my focus starts with "school" and then incorporates "safety" into the picture. In many districts, the "school" is nearly absent in safety planning, and there is far too much crossover of policing into classrooms.

In my view, the future of sustainable safety in schools recognizes that student growth, learning, and socialization must be the foundation on which a safe environment is built; trust between students and the adults with whom they interact is essential to establishing this foundation. Part of that trust is developed through the implicit and explicit actions of adults – and anyone who spends time with children knows that they pick up on the attitudes and emotions of adults within their orbits.

When there is a gun – and by default, the constant threat of violence – between an adult and a child, there is an artificially low ceiling placed on the trust that can grow in the space between. Regardless of whether understood at a surface level, a child who is policed will recognize and react to a barrier, preventing the relationship required for learning and growing.

One suggestion pushed by the National Rifle Association (NRA) and other similarly minded groups and individuals is to arm teachers as a "protective measure" against violence. I cannot stress enough the inappropriateness of such a suggestion. Teachers, already asked to perform miracles in education on always-shrinking resource allocations, should never be *armed against their students*. Rather, a teacher must be available as a mentor and trusted figure and should never be seen as the potential source of violence against their charges.

Taking this concept further as it relates to school support staff, I have to question the wisdom of the common practice of hiring former police officers or military personnel as School Resource Officers. Police and military members receive extensive training, particularly on firearms and security activities. However, such training is based on a relationship between authority and perpetrator or soldier and enemy combatant. Working with young people who are living through physical and emotional changes, emotional regulation adjustments, and a range of other adolescent realities requires a different skillset and mindset, than what is fostered in law enforcement or military training.

Evidence is clear that even those who are trained in dealing with adversarial combatants are not properly equipped to respond in instances of school shootings, ostensibly the primary reason for their presence in schools. The K-12 Shooting Database makes it quite clear that having armed officers in schools is a statistically less effective solution in preventing violence than increased funding for social-emotional and behavioral health professionals in educational settings.

Achieving sustainable change in school safety requires a concerted effort in advocacy and the implementation of supportive policies at various levels. This chapter will explore strategies for building community support, advocating for behavioral health-centered policies, and creating a lasting culture of safety and well-being in schools.

The scope of school violence encompasses a wide spectrum of behaviors that disrupt the learning environment and threaten the well-being of students and staff. Most recognizable are the physical forms of violence – shootings, student fights, corporal punishment – yet other forms are potentially more prevalent. Understanding the various forms that represent the spectrum of violence, the statistical realities, and the profound impacts of violent behaviors is crucial for developing effective prevention and intervention strategies.

In this chapter, I will attempt to delineate the scope of school violence, examine its various manifestations, contrast statistical data with public perceptions, and explore its ripple effects on individuals and the broader school community. I will also explain how I see the interconnectedness of violence *within* schools and the *external* environments of students' homes and communities.

Types of School Violence

School violence as discussed in these pages consists of many harmful acts of varying natures and severities. I will broadly categorize these types of violence as physical, psychological, bullying (including cyberbullying), and hate crimes. *Physical* violence includes acts such as fighting, assault (with or without a weapon), and robbery. *Psychological* violence includes verbal threats, intimidation, and emotional abuse. *Bullying* involves repeated aggressive behavior intended to harm or intimidate; its digital extension, *cyberbullying*, has become increasingly prevalent with the rise of social media and online communication. *Hate crimes* in schools are offenses motivated by an implicit or explicit bias against a victim's perceived race, religion, sexual orientation, or other protected class of characteristics.

Statistical data can help us draw a useful picture of these various forms of violence in United States (U.S.) public schools. I will be presenting the most current publicly available data I have been able to find, including qualitative and quantitative studies, newspaper reporting, and other published literature on the various types of violence in schools.

During the 2021–22 academic year, schools recorded approximately 857,500 violent incidents, including *rape or attempted rape*, sexual *assault* other than rape, *robbery* (with or without a weapon), *physical attacks or fights* (with or without a weapon), and *threat* of physical attack (with or without a weapon). Schools also recorded 479,500 nonviolent incidents that same academic year. A significant majority of schools (67 percent) reported experiencing at least one violent incident, while 59 percent reported at least one nonviolent incident during this period.

Delving into specific types of physical violence, 61 percent of schools reported at least one physical attack or fight *without* a weapon, and 4 percent reported such an attack *with* a weapon. Hate crimes, though less frequent, were still reported by 3 percent (more than 3,000) of all public schools. The occurrence of hate crimes was notably higher (8 percent) in schools with a student population of more than 1,000 students compared to schools with smaller student enrollments, where rates ranged between 2 and 4 percent.

Bullying remains a pervasive issue of significant concern. Data from the 2021-22 school year indicates that bullying at school at least once a week was reported by 28 percent of middle schools, a higher rate than the 15 percent reported by

14

high/secondary schools and 10 percent by elementary/ primary schools. Cyberbullying, occurring either at school or away from school at least once a week, was reported by an even larger proportion of middle schools (37 percent) and high/secondary schools (25 percent), compared to 6 percent of elementary schools. These figures underscore that, while severe, high-profile incidents like school shootings are relatively rare, other forms of violence and aggression are a daily reality for many students.

The ubiquity of these normalized forms of violence necessitates comprehensive prevention strategies to address the full spectrum of harmful behaviors and to foster genuinely safe and supportive learning environments. Failing to address these incidents not only causes immediate harm, but also contributes to a negative school climate and acts as a precursor to more severe forms of violence.

The high incidence of cyberbullying, particularly in middle schools where it surpasses in-school bullying rates, signals a sometimes-invisible shift in the landscape of peer aggression. Virtual communities—Instagram, Snapchat, TikTok, Facebook, Discord, and others—ensure that violence is no longer confined to school grounds or hours which creates the potential for around-the-clock harassment. This unfortunate pervasiveness makes it difficult for victims to escape and can intensify feelings of isolation and distress. Consequently, prevention strategies must evolve to adequately address online safety, digital citizenship, and the unique mental health challenges posed by cyberbullying.

Reality Versus Perception

Public discourse on school violence is often dominated by high-profile incidents of mass violence, particularly school shootings. While these events are undeniably tragic and have devastating consequences, it is essential to examine their statistical reality in contrast to the heightened public fear they often generate. When viewed in comparison to law enforcement data, it becomes apparent that media coverage plays a significant role in shaping these misperceptions.

Statistically, school shootings represent a small fraction of the overall gun violence to which youth are exposed. To illustrate, consider data from countries within the Group of Seven (G7), an international coalition of the world's most industrialized nations, including the U.S., Canada, France, Germany, Italy, Japan, and the United Kingdom. Between 2009 and 2018, the United States averaged six school shootings every two and a half months, a notable and damning contrast to the combined total of five (5) recorded school shootings in the other G-7 countries during the same ten-year period. Despite this comparatively shocking level of violence, multiple-victim youth homicides in schools, though showing an increase since 2009, still accounted for less than 3 percent of all youth homicides in the U.S. between 1994 and 2016. Furthermore, approximately 90 percent of school-related youth homicide incidents involve a single victim, which contradicts the common perception that most school-related homicides are mass shootings.

Media outlets tend to give extensive coverage to rare and sensational events like school shootings – emotionally charged and terrible, yet profitable, events. Since Columbine (see chapter 22), research shows that school shootings resulting in more victim injuries or fatalities, or those committed by perpetrators with prior criminal records or known psychological issues, receive significantly more media attention. Today, school shootings are nearly four times more likely to receive news coverage compared to other types of mass shootings, even though the overwhelming majority (85 percent) of child gun homicides occur in the home, not at school.

Disparities in this media coverage can lead to an *availability bias* in public perception, where vivid and easily recalled events such as school shootings are perceived as more common or representative than they statistically are. This skewed perception can, in turn, influence policy responses and resource allocation, potentially leading to an overemphasis on preventing rare, high-profile events. This misplaced focus comes at the expense of addressing more common forms of school violence or the underlying systemic causes of violence affecting youth. The intense fear generated by the focus on mass school violence can also fuel support for security measures that may not be evidence-based yet offer a visible sense of immediate action.

Focusing the narrative on school shootings also tends to obscure the broader reality of youth victimization. While school safety is paramount, the data indicate that for many children, particularly concerning gun violence, the home and community environments may pose greater risks. Rather than concentrating resources disproportionately on schools as the primary locus of danger, a comprehensive approach to youth violence prevention must acknowledge and address violence across all settings where children live, learn, and play.

The Ripple Effect: Impact on Students, Educators, and School Climate

School violence, in its various forms, creates far-reaching ripples that extend beyond the immediate victims and perpetrators. It profoundly affects the entire school community, impacting students' academic and emotional well-being, educators' professional lives and mental health, and the overall school climate.

Students exposed to violence, whether in their neighborhoods or directly within the school, experience observable negative consequences. Research consistently shows that such exposure leads to reduced school attendance, lower academic achievement, increased misbehavior, and a decreased likelihood of graduating from high school. Students who feel unsafe at school are more likely to report symptoms of depression and see fewer academic successes than peers who feel safe and supported. Children exposed to violence may be psychologically scarred and face an increased risk of mental health problems (e.g., post-traumatic stress disorder, depression, and anxiety), learning disabilities, and other neurocognitive issues. Even witnessing violence can have detrimental effects on student conduct and attitudes toward school. School shootings, in particular, have been shown to result in long-term negative academic, professional (e.g., reduced lifetime earnings), and mental health outcomes for student survivors, including an increased reliance on behavioral health medication.

Educators are also deeply affected by school violence. Student aggression and violence directed towards teachers contributes to heightened stress, anxiety, and burnout, which negatively impacts their physical and mental health. These experiences can then lead to impaired instructional and classroom management practices, lower teaching efficacy, increased absenteeism, and a greater likelihood of teachers transferring to other schools or leaving the profession entirely. Concerns about school shootings are common among current teachers and may even deter prospective teachers from entering the profession. This teacher attrition represents a significant hidden cost of school violence, potentially lowering educational quality and creating instability, especially in schools already facing significant challenges.

The overall school climate suffers immensely in the presence of violence. A positive school climate, characterized by feelings of safety, support, and engagement, is crucial for learning and development. However, violence and the fear it engenders can disrupt this climate, leading to environments where students feel less safe and connected. Research highlights a critical interaction between these elements. Specifically, the negative impact of neighborhood violence on students' academic performance is often exacerbated if they attend schools that are also perceived as unsafe or lacking a strong sense of community. Conversely, a positive and supportive school climate can act as a buffer, mitigating some of the detrimental effects of external stressors. This underscores that school violence prevention efforts must be multifaceted, addressing incidents within the school while also actively working to cultivate an environment that helps students cope with adversities originating beyond school walls.

The Interconnectedness of School, Community, and Home Environments in Violence

Violence within schools is rarely an isolated phenomenon; it is often deeply intertwined with, and influenced by, factors present in students' homes and the broader community. Given this reality, we must recognize that schools do not exist in a vacuum, and the challenges faced by students while not in school frequently spill over into the educational environment, impacting behavior, safety, and learning.

Research consistently demonstrates that neighborhood characteristics play a significant role in shaping the context of school violence. Factors such as neighborhood socioeconomic disadvantage, including poverty and lack of opportunity, are strongly correlated with higher rates of youth violence perpetration. Social disorganization theory posits that neighborhood instability—characterized by low socioeconomic status, ethnic heterogeneity, and high residential mobility—can lead to weakened social control and, consequently, higher levels of violence. These community-level stressors can create an environment where violence is more prevalent and may even be normalized, influencing the behavior of young people both within their neighborhoods and at school.

Exposure to community violence has a direct and detrimental impact on students, and is linked to psychological distress, impaired concentration, and negative academic outcomes. Recent neurological studies indicate that living in neighborhoods with high levels of violence can affect brain development in young people. For instance, a particularly prominent area of concern is the development of the amygdala, a region of the brain involved in emotional regulation and threat response. This heightened threat perception can manifest in school as hypervigilance, anxiety, aggression, or difficulty focusing, contributing to behavioral issues and potentially increasing the likelihood of involvement in violent incidents. This physiological impact underscores the necessity for trauma-informed practices within schools that recognize and address the deep-seated effects of community violence exposure, rather than merely responding punitively to the resulting behaviors.

The relationship between school and community violence is often bi-directional. Conflicts that originate in the neighborhood can spill into the school, and vice versa. Of equal importance is the potential for schools to act as protective environments beyond the confines of the educational environment. Strong school-community partnerships and effective in-school support systems help to mitigate the negative impacts of community violence on students. This suggests that school violence prevention strategies should extend beyond the physical restraints of school grounds to involve collaborative efforts with community organizations, families, and local agencies to address the root causes of violence in the broader environment. Caregiver nurturance has also been identified as a buffer against the harmful effects of community violence on brain development, highlighting the importance of family support systems.

As demonstrated in this chapter, the landscape of school violence includes many forms and contributing factors. We have also seen how effective collaboration can be helpful both within and out of school settings. In the next chapter, we will look at what is understood about the causes and contributing factors of our current violent epidemic.

Chapter 2: Root Causes and Contributing Factors

There are several models for behavior and development that can be applied to understand the factors that run beneath and through the modern crisis of school violence. Abraham Maslow and Urie Bronfenbrenner are perhaps the best-known examples of such models, as their respective Hierarchy of Needs and Ecological Systems Theory are among the most referenced works in modern social sciences.

In my view, however, the most appropriate lens through which to view the relationship between safety policy and continuing violence is through the more recent Polyvagal Theory (PVT), first explained by Dr. Stephen Porges in his 1995 paper, *Orienting in a defensive world: mammalian modifications of our evolutionary heritage.* Porges' theory explores behavior as a collection of evolutionary, neuroscientific, and psychological factors that alter how the Vagus nerve functions in emotion regulation, social connection and fear response. As PVT directly addresses stress, fear, and acute stress responses, this framework can be enlightening when applied to schools, armed security, and violence.

In this chapter, I will reflect on the underlying conditions of school violence using the frameworks described by both Porges and Bronfenbrenner, attempting to illustrate how the two overlap and intertwine in the lived experience of contemporary students.

Individual Risk Factors

Individual-level factors can significantly elevate a student's risk of engaging in or being affected by school violence. Among these, mental health conditions, exposure to trauma, and pre-existing behavioral issues are prominent. In his book "Rampage Nation: Securing America from Mass Shootings," Louis Klarevas explains that perpetrators of mass shootings are often men of working age who experience mental health challenges, frequently characterized by a volatile combination of high self-esteem and acute sensitivity to criticism or perceived ridicule.

It is crucial to understand that "mental health issues" is a broad term and does not equate to a specific diagnosis of severe mental illness as the sole cause of such extreme violence. Public discourse, importantly, oversimplifies this link, potentially stigmatizing individuals with even minor or undiagnosed mental health conditions. The reality is that a confluence of factors, including psychological states, social grievances, and access to lethal means, typically contributes to such acts.

Exposure to violence—whether in the home, community, or school—is a profound traumatic experience that can have lasting neurocognitive and behavioral consequences for children. Such exposure increases the risk of developing mental health problems, including Post-Traumatic Stress Disorder (PTSD), depression, and anxiety, as well as learning disabilities. These conditions, in turn, can manifest as behavioral problems in school, poorer academic performance, and increased absenteeism.

If these behaviors are not viewed through a trauma-informed lens, they may be misconstrued as defiance or aggression, leading to punitive responses rather than the necessary supportive interventions. This highlights the critical need for schools to adopt trauma-informed approaches that can identify and support students whose actions may be a manifestation of underlying trauma.

From a polyvagal perspective, chronic stress, trauma, and unaddressed mental health conditions can lead to a dysregulated autonomic nervous system. Individuals frequently experiencing trauma may spend extended periods in a sympathetic fight/flight state, which may manifest as defiance or aggression. The trauma-sensitive nervous system, under these conditions, is constantly preparing for danger.

If fight/flight is not an option or if the system is overwhelmed, the individual may collapse into a *dorsal vagal freeze* or *shutdown state* which often presents outwardly as withdrawal, disengagement, or even result in decreased academic performance and increased absenteeism. These reactions to stress represent a more primitive immobilization response to perceived overwhelming threat.

Louis Klarevas's observation that perpetrators with "high self-esteem and acute sensitivity to criticism or perceived ridicule," can be viewed through the PVT lens as a rigid sympathetic activation, where perceived threats (criticism) immediately trigger a defensive, fight-oriented response to protect a fragile sense of self, making it difficult to access the calming influence of the ventral vagal system and preventing access to executive decision-making centers within the brain.

Due to these conflicting responses to stress and trauma, there is a critical need for schools to adopt trauma-informed approaches, as trauma-induced behaviors might otherwise be erroneously identified as defiance or aggression. Polyvagal theory explains why this lens is crucial: if a student's nervous system is stuck in fight/flight or freeze due to trauma, punitive responses will only further activate their defensive states, making them feel less safe and more dysregulated, and unreceptive to learning or relationship-building opportunities.

Instead of fostering safety with ventral vagal stimulation, it reinforces threat by activating the sympathetic dorsal vagal.

Peer and Social Dynamics

The social ecosystem of a school, particularly peer interactions, plays a significant role in the landscape of school violence. Bullying, in its various forms, remains a pervasive issue. National data indicate that 28 percent of middle schools report that bullying occurs at least once a week. The consequences of bullying extend to both victims and perpetrators, with those who bully others being at an increased risk for substance misuse, academic difficulties, and engagement in violence later in life. While media narratives sometimes simplistically link bullying to extreme acts of violence like school shootings, it is more accurately understood as a complex contributing stressor within a large and complex constellation of factors, rather than the sole, direct cause.

Gang involvement also contributes to school violence, often reflecting broader community dynamics where deviant peer groups influence antisocial behavior. Social exclusion, the experience of being ostracized or marginalized by peers, can be a potent psychological stressor for adolescents, potentially leading to feelings of isolation, anger, and resentment that may, in some instances, contribute to aggressive or withdrawn behaviors.

As mentioned previously, the advent of social media has further complicated these peer dynamics. The high rates of cyberbullying reported, especially in middle schools, indicate that peer aggression and exclusion are now so pervasive as to be inescapable.

Bullying, cyberbullying, and social exclusion are academically and popularly understood as potent psychological stressors. From a polyvagal perspective, these experiences directly impact *neuroception* – the unconscious process by which the nervous system evaluates risk in the environment.

Being bullied or ostracized signals danger, triggering a move down the polyvagal ladder towards sympathetic activation (anxiety, anger, resentment) or dorsal vagal shutdown (isolation, withdrawal). The "inescapable" nature of cyberbullying means the threats are constant, giving few opportunities for the nervous system to return to a state of safety. The resulting social exclusion can be a potent psychological stressor for adolescents, potentially leading to feelings of isolation, anger, and resentment that may, in some instances, contribute to aggressive or withdrawn behaviors. These represent classic polyvagal responses: anger and aggression as sympathetic fight, isolation and withdrawal as dorsal vagal freeze.

Deviant peer groups and gang involvement can provide a sense of belonging and protection for individuals whose nervous systems perceive the broader environment to be threatening. While not a healthy coping mechanism, joining a gang might, paradoxically, offer the perception of safety by providing a social hierarchy and a collective defense against external threats, creating a shared and distorted form of social engagement.

In addition, exposure to community violence or a personal history of socioeconomic disadvantage are factors that create chronic stress and unrelenting perceptions of threat, impacting the collective nervous system of a community. Children growing up in such environments are constantly in a state of hypervigilance (sympathetic activation) or shutdown (dorsal vagal), impairing their ability to learn, regulate emotions, and form secure attachments.

Polyvagal dysregulation can be seen in a widespread environmental context as triggering defensive states, making individuals increasingly prone to aggression or disengagement. The easy accessibility of weapons in the United States significantly increases the potential for lethality in communities with chronically engaged fight responses.

Within the sphere of Vagal responses, individual awareness of easily accessible lethality unconsciously amplifies the perceived threat within the environment. For an individual already struggling with dysregulation, the immediate availability of a weapon can quickly shift their nervous system from a state of distress to an impulsive, extreme sympathetic fight response, leading to devastating outcomes. The perception of extreme threat is capable of overriding any potential for ventral vagal regulation.

School Environment and the Ventral Vagal State

The school environment itself, encompassing its overall climate, disciplinary approaches, and academic pressures, can either serve as a protective factor against violence or inadvertently contribute to its occurrence. A positive school climate, characterized by safety, mutual respect, strong student-teacher relationships, and a sense of belonging, is fundamental to violence prevention. Such an environment fosters pro-social behavior and can buffer students against external stressors.

Conversely, punitive and inconsistently applied disciplinary policies can undermine school safety and student well-being. Zero-tolerance policies, often implemented with the intention of creating safer schools by removing students perceived as disruptive, have come under significant criticism. Research suggests these policies are largely ineffective at deterring the behaviors they target and may even exacerbate them, particularly for students who are repeatedly suspended. This creates a paradox where measures intended to enhance safety may, in fact, contribute to a cycle of exclusion and disengagement, potentially increasing long-term risks.

Furthermore, the school climate can act as a crucial modulator of external stressors. Studies have shown that a positive school climate can mitigate the negative academic impacts of exposure to neighborhood violence. This indicates that the school environment is not merely a passive recipient of community influences but can actively shape students' resilience and coping mechanisms. Therefore, investments in improving school climate, through strategies such as Social and Emotional Learning (SEL) and restorative practices, represent direct investments in violence prevention and overall student success. High academic stress, without adequate support systems, can also contribute to student anxiety and maladaptive coping behaviors, further underscoring the need for a balanced and supportive school environment.

Punitive and Inconsistent Disciplinary Policies

Policies and environments focused on punitive discipline run counter to the desired outcomes seen in spaces where SEL and trauma-informed practices are the standard. While they are ostensibly intended to increase safety and reduce hard, zero-tolerance policies instead undermine the fabric of school safety.

Zero-tolerance policies create an environment of unpredictability and fear for students, particularly those who are already struggling with trauma or a lack of emotional support outside of school. These policies create a constant threat of danger, pushing students into an unrelenting state of low sympathetic (fight/flight) or dorsal vagal (freeze/shutdown) states, especially if they are already dysregulated due to trauma.

Research shows that these policies are generally ineffective in deterring the behaviors they claim to prevent. For students who frequently receive punishment under these policies, the problems are exacerbated rather than alleviated. From a polyvagal perspective, punitive measures that do not account for the underlying polyvagal state do not help students regulate; they reinforce the perception of threat, leading to increased defensive behaviors.

This cycle of exclusion and disengagement aligns with a dorsal vagal collapse, where students are removed from the learning environment, further isolating them and reducing opportunities for ventral vagal connection and co-regulation.

School-to-Prison Pipeline and Chronic Dysregulation

Zero-tolerance policies in schools, which mandate predetermined, often severe, consequences for specific student infractions, regardless of context or mitigating circumstances, have been a significant feature of school discipline landscapes, particularly since the federal Gun-Free Schools Act of 1994. These policies, initially targeting weapons possession, quickly expanded to cover a wide array of behaviors, including minor offenses and subjective infractions like "defiance" or "disrespect."

While proponents argue that zero-tolerance policies create safer and more orderly learning environments by unequivocally deterring misbehavior, a substantial body of research challenges this assertion. Studies indicate that these policies do not effectively deter the behaviors they are designed to punish and, in some cases, may even lead to increased suspensions rather than reducing their frequency.

This suggests a fundamental flaw in the deterrence theory underpinning such policies, likely because they fail to address the underlying causes of student misbehavior, such as trauma, mental health needs, or undeveloped social-emotional skills, opting instead for purely punitive responses.

A major criticism of zero-tolerance policies is their disproportionate impact on already marginalized student populations. Research consistently shows that Black and Brown students, as well as students with disabilities, are suspended and expelled at significantly higher rates than their peers for similar offenses under these policies. For example, data from Virginia's 2011-2012 school year showed that while Black students made up 23 percent of total enrollment, they accounted for a much larger proportion of short- and long-term suspensions and expulsions. Such disparities suggest that even if policies are superficially neutral, their application is influenced by explicit or implicit biases of individuals within school systems, leading to inequitable outcomes.

The widespread use of exclusionary discipline (suspensions and expulsions) under zero-tolerance regimes is a primary driver of the school-to-prison pipeline – the process by which students, particularly those from disadvantaged backgrounds and minority groups, become involved with the juvenile and criminal justice systems due to non-criminal behavior. Suspensions and expulsions remove students from the learning environment, increasing their risk of academic failure, dropout, and subsequent involvement with the legal system. The criminalization of developmentally appropriate student behavior, where minor school infractions are treated as matters for law enforcement, further enhances this pipeline.

The school-to-prison pipeline an illustrative manifestation of polyvagal dysregulation. By criminalizing developmentally appropriate student behavior and relying heavily on exclusionary discipline, schools counterintuitively contribute to a cycle where students, often those whose nervous systems are already chronically in defensive states due to trauma or disadvantage, are further pushed into isolation and criminalization.

Removing students from their learning environments, removing the structure and support found within, increases their risk of academic failure, dropout, and potential for involvement with the justice system. Therefore, exclusionary discipline perpetuates dorsal vagal shutdown and further entrenches them in a state of disconnection and vulnerability. Their opportunities for ventral vagal connection, co-regulation, and a sense of safety are systematically removed. Whatever gains may be intended through this action are negated by the increased dysregulation of the experience.

Further, the disproportionate impact of exclusionary discipline on marginalized student populations suggests that systemic biases lead to a misinterpretation of their polyvagal states, often labeling defensive reactions as defiance rather than distress, thus reinforcing their descent down the polyvagal ladder and increasing long-term justice system involvement.

In essence, Polyvagal Theory provides a framework for understanding how the various individual, peer, school, and societal factors impact the nervous system's capacity for internalizing safety, connection, and regulation. It highlights that school violence and the school-to-prison pipeline are not merely behavioral problems but often represent manifestations of deeply rooted physiological and psychological responses to perceived threats and chronic dysregulation, underscoring the need for interventions that prioritize safety, connection, and co-regulation to foster more resilient and prosocial behaviors.

Chapter 3: Cultivating Comprehensive Safety for Thriving Schools

The conversation surrounding school safety in our nation has, for too long, been dominated by a reactive posture, a response to tragedy that often prioritizes physical fortification over the foundational elements of what I see as a truly secure and nurturing learning environment. While the instinct to protect our children is understandable (as a father of three public school students, I get it), the methods we choose must be guided by evidence, wisdom, and a holistic understanding of what truly makes a school safe. This text argues for such a paradigm shift—a move away from an overreliance on measures that harden our schools physically but may inadvertently chill their climate, towards an embrace of comprehensive strategies that cultivate the social, emotional, and psychological well-being of every student and staff member.

The call to reimagine school safety is not a call to diminish its importance; rather, it is an invitation to broaden our collective perspective. True safety is more than the absence of violence; it is the presence of a supportive community, a climate of trust and respect, and the availability of resources that empower students to navigate challenges and flourish. It is about creating schools where learning is not just about academics but about developing the whole child as a member of the community and establishing the foundation upon which those children grown into adults. The path to such schools requires a collective commitment—from parents and educators to policymakers and community leaders—to invest in proactive, preventative, and person-centered approaches. This work champions that holistic vision, offering a roadmap towards creating educational spaces where all children feel secure, valued, and ready to achieve their full potential. The arguments presented herein are grounded in research and animated by a deep belief in the transformative power of schools designed not just to prevent the worst, but to nurture the best in every child.

The Current Over-reliance on Punitive Measures and Armed Security

The prevailing response to concerns about school safety has often centered on visible, physical security enhancements and punitive disciplinary policies. This includes the proliferation of surveillance technologies, such as security cameras and AI-based behavior or weapons detection systems, and an increased presence of armed personnel, whether School Resource Officers (SROs – often retired police or military personnel) or private security guards. Coupled with this is the widespread adoption of zero-tolerance policies, which mandate strict, often exclusionary, consequences for student misbehavior.

While these measures are frequently implemented with the intention of deterring violence and maintaining order, their effectiveness is increasingly questioned, and their potential for negative consequences is significant. Research suggests that the presence of armed officers often has "no impact" on overall school safety or day-to-day crime and may not prevent mass casualty events. In fact, most school shootings with mass casualties occurred in schools that already had armed personnel on campus or nearby, along with other security measures like cameras and electronic monitoring. Furthermore, there is "little evidence to prove that any of these companies' claims are true" regarding the efficacy of advanced surveillance technologies like AI-based weapons detection.

Instead of enhancing safety, such measures can contribute to a punitive school environment where students, particularly students of color and those with disabilities, are more likely to be arrested, suspended, or expelled for age-appropriate, non-criminal, or non-violent behavior. This heightened monitoring and disciplinary action can foster a climate of fear and mistrust, undermining the very sense of safety these measures aim to create. Students may feel constantly watched, which prevents them from fully trusting their educators, and hinders their ability to express themselves. This dynamic can exacerbate existing racial biases in school discipline, contributing to the "school-to-prison pipeline" by increasing early exposure to punitive and exclusionary discipline, which is linked to poorer academic performance and greater involvement with the criminal justice system.

Case studies further illustrate how a singular focus on physical security can lead to the neglect of other critical educational goals, such as academic engagement and the cultivation of a positive school culture. The financial investment in these security measures also diverts resources from support like classroom teachers, paraeducators, special education professionals, counselors, social workers, and school psychologists, which are essential for addressing the root causes of student distress and behavior. True school safety develops culturally responsive programming and curriculum are fully funded, not from these hardening security measures. The prevailing narrative that equates visible security with actual safety appears to be a misconception, potentially leading to environments that are objectively less safe for students, while giving parents and other caregivers the illusion of safety. Meanwhile, districts across the country continue to divert resources from more effective, supportive strategies.

A Multi-Layered, Proactive Approach

In contrast to the reactive and often narrowly focused security models, holistic school safety offers a multi-layered, proactive, and comprehensive framework. This approach recognizes that genuine safety is built on a foundation of positive relationships, emotional well-being, and a supportive community, rather than solely on physical deterrents. It involves more than just taking the easy steps that make families feel superficially protected. It is important to implement appropriate security technologies, but without also fostering strong community relationships and prioritizing mental wellness, our safety plans will be nothing more than reactive to violence already in progress.

A positive school climate, the "quality and character of school life," encompassing the school environment, student and school safety (both physical and emotional), and the active involvement of the entire school community is at the heart of holistic safety. It is about creating conditions where students and staff feel safe, supported, respected, and engaged.

Building this environment involves a spectrum of services from universal prevention and mental health literacy for all students to targeted interventions for those at risk, and intensive support for students with significant needs. It includes early intervention, trauma-informed practices, and crisis intervention systems.

Holistic safety requires a top-down commitment and a culture of collaboration where every adult in the school building—from administrators and teachers to counselors, support staff, and even bus drivers—understands their role in creating a safe and welcoming environment.

Instead of relying primarily on punitive discipline, holistic safety and positive climates rely on restorative approaches that focus on repairing harm, building community, and teaching conflict resolution skills, holding students accountable in a supportive manner that maintains and enhances relationships.

In order to build a climate that survives beyond a single administration, meaningful engagement with parents and deep collaboration with community organizations, including mental health providers and, where appropriate, law enforcement in supportive, non-punitive roles, are crucial for creating a comprehensive network of support around students.

In a world where holistic safety is the norm, students are viewed as valuable resources in safety planning, with their insights and participation actively sought to enhance the effectiveness of safety measures and foster a sense of ownership.

Ohio's Comprehensive School Safety Framework exemplifies such an approach, emphasizing both emotional and physical safety through the engagement of school staff, students, families, and the community, integrating social-emotional learning (SEL) and behavioral health supports. This ecosystem approach underscores that holistic safety is about cultivating a pervasive *culture* of safety and support, rather than implementing isolated programs.

Student Well-being, Equity, and Academic Success

Adopting a holistic approach to school safety is not merely an alternative strategy; it is a fundamental necessity for fostering environments where students can truly flourish. The benefits extend far beyond the prevention of violence, profoundly impacting student mental health, academic achievement, and the creation of a more equitable school experience for all.

A positive school climate, a cornerstone of holistic safety, is directly linked to improved student outcomes, including attendance rates, test scores, and graduation rates. When students feel safe, supported, valued, and engaged, they are more invested in participation, and better able to focus on learning. Mental health supports, such as access to counselors, social-emotional learning (SEL) programs, and restorative practices, empower students to be engaged in their learning, and to build healthy relationships that contribute to their own positive climate and safe environment. These supports have been shown to reduce disciplinary incidents, improve teachers' perceptions of school climate, and increasing academic achievement.

Furthermore, holistic approaches can significantly advance equity. Punitive measures and an overreliance on security personnel disproportionately affect students of color and students with disabilities, leading to higher rates of suspension, expulsion, and arrest. This early exposure to exclusionary discipline can derail educational trajectories and limit future opportunities. By contrast, holistic strategies like restorative justice and robust mental health services aim to address the root causes of behavior and provide support rather than punishment, thereby reducing these disparities and fostering a more inclusive environment where all students have the opportunity to succeed. Investing in holistic safety is, therefore, not a diversion from academic goals but an essential prerequisite for achieving them, creating a positive feedback loop where well-being and learning reinforce each other.

This introduction has laid the groundwork for a deeper exploration of holistic school safety. The subsequent chapters will delve into the foundational elements of this approach, examine its key pillars in action, and provide guidance on policy, funding, and advocacy to make holistic safety a reality in every school.

Chapter 4: The NRA's Role in Promoting School Violence

Before moving on, it is vital to address the gun-toting elephant in the room. The shape of school-related gun violence cannot be understood without grasping how the National Rifle Association (NRA) has reshaped our public discourse.

The NRA stands as a pivotal and frequently debated voice in shaping American gun policy. From its inception in 1871 as an organization dedicated to promoting marksmanship, the NRA has undergone a significant transformation. While it still offers marksmanship training and certification, it has evolved to a primary focus on political action, exerting considerable influence over gun laws in the United States. Here, we will explore the NRA's journey, actions, and impact on the legal and political discourse surrounding firearms.

In this chapter, we will look briefly at the NRA's origins and transformation, and its involvement in shaping gun control legislation at both federal and state levels. Most importantly, we will see how it has successfully reshaped popular understanding of the Second Amendment, and how it has influenced the Supreme Court on landmark cases that have made true school or community safety achievement such an uphill challenge. Ultimately, I hope to offer a useful understanding of the NRA's continuing role in the prevention of common-sense legislation in the promotion of public safety.

The NRA's Transformation

The NRA was founded in 1871 by Union Army veterans Colonel William C. Church and General George Wingate, who were concerned about the apparent lack of marksmanship skills displayed by Union troops during the Civil War. Their primary objective was to "promote and encourage rifle shooting on a scientific basis," as articulated by Church in a magazine editorial. In its early years, the promoted sport shooting and improved firearm proficiency. The NRA also established and promoted the importance of marksmanship among youth, initiating programs in the early 1900s to encourage shooting sports in colleges, universities, and military academies. This dedication extended to the military, with the NRA setting standards for military rifle training, even inspiring the federal government to establish a division within the War Department focused on promoting rifle practice among soldiers and civilians alike.

The American NRA was modeled after the National Rifle Association in Great Britain, which had been formed in 1859, indicating an international context for its initial goals. The early emphasis on skill development and national preparedness suggests a foundational mission rooted in practical concerns rather than ideological advocacy for gun rights. The founders, being military men, were likely driven by a desire to enhance the effectiveness of the nation's armed forces and promote responsible firearm handling. The activities undertaken during this period—training, competitions, and establishing ranges—were all geared towards improving shooting proficiency, without the political lobbying that defines the organization today.

Over time, the NRA's focus shifted, incorporating legislative affairs into its activities. This change of priority became more pronounced following the passage of the National Firearms Act of 1934, the first federal gun control law in the U.S. The NRA formed its Legislative Affairs Division to inform its members about upcoming firearm-related bills, marking its initial step into the political arena. In stark contrast to its modern approach, the NRA *supported* some early gun control measures, including the Federal Firearms Act of 1938 and the Gun Control Act of 1968. In 1939, the NRA's president, Karl T. Frederick, testified before Congress in support of *restricting the general practice of carrying weapons*, advocating for licensing. Similarly, after the assassination of President John F. Kennedy in 1963, the NRA's executive vice-president, Franklin Orth, agreed that mail-order sales of firearms must be banned, stating that "no sane American" could object to such a measure.

The Gun Control Act of 1968, passed in the wake of further assassinations and civil unrest, also received support from the NRA, with a spokesman indicating that the "sportsmen of America" could live with the measure, despite some restrictive portions. During this period, however, internal tensions were growing within the organization. Several members began to advocate for a stronger defense of gun ownership rights, establishing a divergence from the organization's more tolerant stance on regulations. This represents the demarcation line between its support of regulation and the organization's current unwavering opposition to virtually all forms of gun control.

Perhaps the most decisive moment in the NRA's history occurred at its 1977 annual convention in Cincinnati, Ohio. What became known as the "Revolt at Cincinnati" or the

"Cincinnati Coup," marked a decisive shift in the organization's direction, fully moving it away from its traditional focus on hunting, conservation, and marksmanship towards its emphasis on defending the right to keep and bear arms. A grassroots movement, spearheaded by Harlon Carter and Neal Knox, successfully challenged the "Old Guard" leadership, who were perceived as being too moderate in their approach to gun control. NRA leadership desired to move the headquarters out of the Washington, D.C. area to Colorado, which many members saw as a retreat from the political arena. The core motivation, however, seems to have been a growing sentiment among a significant portion of the membership that the NRA needed to adopt a more assertive and uncompromising stance against gun control legislation.

Harlon Carter, who had previously served as the first head of the NRA's lobbying arm, the Institute for Legislative Action (ILA), played a central role in the revolt, advocating for a "no compromise" approach to gun legislation, believing that any restrictions on gun ownership were unacceptable. Neal Knox, a gun rights activist and editor of Rifle magazine, also proved instrumental in raising support for the movement through his publications, urging readers towards political action. The "Revolt at Cincinnati" resulted in Carter replacing Maxwell Rich as the executive vice president and Knox taking over the NRA-ILA. Here was the fundamental ideological realignment within the NRA: gone was its marksmanship mission, replaced by its identity as a no-exceptions defender of Second Amendment rights. From this point forward, the NRA was primarily set on political activism aimed at opposing virtually any legislative proposal for firearm control.

Prior to the "Revolt at Cincinnati," the NRA's relationship with gun control legislation was more flexible, even including periods of support. Notably, the NRA played a role in the drafting and support of the National Firearms Act (NFA) of 1934, which aimed to regulate certain types of firearms associated with criminal activity during the Prohibition era, including machine guns and sawed-off shotguns, through taxation and registration requirements. The NRA initially opposed the NFA, but gave its support after amendments to remove pistols and revolvers from its purview and a redefinition of "machine gun" were made. The NRA also supported the Federal Firearms Act of 1938, which aimed to prevent convicted felons from accessing firearms. The NRA also initially backed the Gun Control Act (GCA) of 1968. This landmark piece of legislation regulated interstate firearms sales, prohibited sales to certain categories of individuals (felons, drug users, and the mentally incompetent), and established a system for licensing gun dealers.

During congressional hearings on the GCA, Orth gave his support for banning mail-order sales of firearms, which was included in the final act. The NRA's motivations for supporting these early gun control measures may have come from a desire to regulate firearms perceived as particularly dangerous or misused by criminals, while also maintaining the rights of law-abiding citizens for sport and self-defense. This historical alignment with certain gun control efforts demonstrates just how much the NRA's modern stance of near-absolute opposition to any new firearm regulations has changed.

After 1977, the NRA adopted a dramatically different and oppositional stance towards nearly all forms of gun control legislation. Characterizing such measures as "infringements upon the Second Amendment rights of law-abiding citizens," the NRA became a vocal and powerful opponent of initiatives aimed at restricting firearm access. This unwavering opposition was on full display in the NRA's 1993 fight against the Brady Handgun Violence Prevention Act, which mandated federal background checks for firearm purchases from licensed dealers and imposed a waiting period for firearm purchases. While the NRA did not outwardly oppose the concept of any system of background checks, it did strongly resist the waiting period requirement. In 1994, the NRA vehemently opposed the Federal Assault Weapons Ban, which prohibited the manufacture and sale of certain semi-automatic firearms and large-capacity magazines for civilian use. The NRA argued that these "assault weapons" were used in a small percentage of crimes and were popular among law-abiding gun owners for sport and self-defense.

One significant legislative victory for the NRA came with the 2005 passage of the Protection of Lawful Commerce in Arms Act (PLCAA). This act shielded gun manufacturers and dealers from most lawsuits resulting from the criminal misuse of their products after purchase. The NRA actively lobbied for the PLCAA because it was crucial to their agenda of protecting the firearms industry from what it considered to be frivolous and politically motivated lawsuits.

In the context of increasing concerns about gun violence in schools, the NRA has unwaveringly advocated for solutions that prioritize increasing the presence of firearms. They lobby for security measures that require armed personnel rather than responsibly restricting access to firearms or evidence-based measures. A recurring proposal from the NRA in response to school shootings has been to increase the number of armed security guards in schools.

The NRA has on many occasions supported the idea of training and arming teachers, arguing that "the only way to stop a bad guy with a gun is with a good guy with a gun". This stance aligns with the NRA's broader philosophy of empowering law-abiding citizens to defend themselves. To promote gun safety among children, the NRA developed the Eddie Eagle GunSafe program, purporting to teach children from pre-kindergarten through the third grade what to do if they encounter a gun: stop, don't touch, run away, and tell a grown-up. The NRA generally opposes gun-free school zones, viewing them as vulnerable "soft targets" for potential attackers. Instead, the organization emphasizes an approach to school safety (the NRA School Shield program) that includes "best practices in security infrastructure, technology, personnel, training, and policy." The NRA's focus on *hardening* schools as targets and promoting firearm safety education for children reflects its core belief that responsible gun ownership and security measures are more effective in preventing school violence than any other method, regardless of what can be empirically demonstrated.

Interpreting the Second Amendment

The full text of the Second Amendment to the U.S. Constitution reads, "A well-regulated Militia, being necessary to the security of a free State, the right of the people to keep and bear Arms, shall not be infringed."

This single sentence has been the subject of extensive debate regarding its original meaning and scope. Historically, two primary interpretations have emerged. The "collective rights" view posits that the Second Amendment primarily protects the right of states to maintain a well-regulated militia (the National Guard in today's structure), suggesting that the right to bear arms is tied to military service within such a militia.

This interpretation emphasizes the prefatory clause regarding the *militia*. Conversely, the "individual rights" view asserts that the Second Amendment guarantees an *individual's* right to own firearms for purposes such as self-defense, independent of service in a militia. The phrase "well-regulated militia" in the Second Amendment has also been subject to varying interpretations.

In the 18th century, "well-regulated" meant well-organized, well-armed, and well-disciplined, rather than subject to extensive government regulation in the modern sense. Historically, citizens were often expected to own arms for potential militia service, reflecting the concept of a citizen militia as a safeguard against a standing army and potential government tyranny. The changing understanding of these key phrases underscores the perceived ambiguity within the Second Amendment's text, allowing alternate interpretations to gain prominence over time.

Particularly after the 1977 revolt, the NRA played a pivotal role in promoting and solidifying the interpretation of the Second Amendment as guaranteeing an *individual* right to own firearms for self-defense, regardless of militia service. This interpretation became the focal point of the NRA's advocacy and public messaging. The organization actively engaged in revisionist legal scholarship, supporting research and publications that advanced the individual rights view.

This included funding essay contests and creating groups like "Academics for the Second Amendment" to bolster the supposed intellectual foundation for their interpretation. The NRA's publications, such as American Rifleman, also served as platforms to disseminate this understanding of the Second Amendment to its members and the broader public.

The interpretation championed by the NRA stands in contrast to earlier understandings of the Second Amendment, including interpretations reflected in early court rulings. For instance, prior to the late 20th century, legal scholarship concluded that the Second Amendment *did not guarantee an individual right to a gun* outside the context of a militia. The NRA's successful advocacy for the individual rights interpretation and reframing of public understanding of the Constitutional right has been instrumental in its ability to oppose gun control measures by framing them as direct infringements on a fundamental Constitutional Right.

The NRA's effective promotion of the "individual rights" interpretation of the Second Amendment has fundamentally changed how the public, legal scholars, and political figures engage in discourse surrounding gun policy. This interpretation has resonated with a substantial portion of the American public and has become a cornerstone of the modern Republican Party's platform on gun rights.

The NRA's influence extends even further, including judicial appointments, with the organization having access to lawmakers and often allowed to weigh in on the suitability of candidates for judgeships based on their views on the Second Amendment. Furthermore, the NRA has been highly successful in framing gun control debates around the Second Amendment, portraying any form of regulation as a violation of their asserted fundamental right to self-defense.

This reframing has created a rhetorical and legal barrier to the passage of protective gun laws, as any proposed restriction is immediately met with the argument that it infringes upon a constitutionally protected individual liberty. By shaping the narrative around gun rights in this manner, the NRA has exerted considerable influence over the potential of any new gun policies in the United States.

Shaping the Legal Landscape of Gun Rights

Possibly surprising to many Americans, the first Supreme Court ruling that upheld the "individual rights" interpretation of the Second Amendment came in 2008, following several previous rulings in favor of the "collective rights" interpretation.

The 1939 Supreme Court case "U.S. v. Miller" arose from a challenge to the National Firearms Act (NFA) of 1934. Jack Miller and Frank Layton were charged with transporting an unregistered sawed-off double-barrel shotgun across state lines, violating the NFA. They argued that the NFA infringed upon their Second Amendment right to keep and bear arms.

The Supreme Court, in a unanimous decision, reversed the district court's dismissal of the charges, holding that the *Second Amendment does not guarantee an individual the right to keep and bear* a sawed-off double-barrel shotgun. Justice James Clark McReynolds, writing for the Court, reasoned that possessing a sawed-off shotgun with a barrel length of less than eighteen inches did not have a reasonable relationship to the preservation or efficiency of a "well-regulated militia".

Historically, this ruling was widely interpreted as supporting the "collective rights" view of the Second

Amendment, suggesting that the right to bear arms was primarily connected to the maintenance of state militias. The Court's emphasis on the relationship between the firearm and a well-regulated militia limited the scope of the Second Amendment's protection to weapons suitable for military use. In later years, as the NRA increasingly advocated for the "individual right," it attempted to include the Miller ruling in this interpretation by arguing that the case only limited the type of weapon protected to those in common use for lawful purposes, including self-defense.

    The Supreme Court case of "District of Columbia v. Heller" in 2008 involved a direct challenge to a gun control law in Washington, D.C., banning the possession of handguns and requiring lawfully owned firearms in the home to be kept unloaded and either disassembled or secured with a trigger lock. Dick Heller, a special police officer in D.C., sued the city, arguing that these regulations violated his Second Amendment right to keep a functional firearm in his home for self-defense. In a 5-4 decision authored by Justice Antonin Scalia, the Supreme Court ruled in favor of Heller, and that the Second Amendment protects an individual's right to possess firearms for traditionally lawful purposes, such as self-defense within the home. The Court reasoned that the Second Amendment's prefatory clause ("A well-regulated Militia...") announces a purpose but does not limit the scope of the operative clause ("the right of the people to keep and bear Arms shall not be infringed"), which connotes an individual right.

    While affirming this individual right, the Court also acknowledged that it is not unlimited, noting that long-standing prohibitions on firearm possession by felons and the mentally ill, as well as laws forbidding the carrying of firearms in sensitive places like schools and government buildings, are presumptively lawful. The NRA played a significant role in advocating for Heller in this case and celebrated the ruling as a monumental victory for gun rights, as it firmly established (and for the first time) the individual right to bear arms as a central component of the Second Amendment.

In 2010, building upon the Heller decision, the NRA lobbied for the Supreme Court to address the applicability of the Second Amendment to state and local governments. The case of "McDonald v. Chicago involved a challenge to a Chicago ordinance that effectively banned handgun possession by private citizens. Otis McDonald and other Chicago residents argued that the Second Amendment right to bear arms, as a direct connection to Heller, should also apply to state and local laws through the Fourteenth Amendment. In another 5-4 decision, the Supreme Court reversed the Seventh Circuit's ruling, holding that the Second Amendment right recognized in Heller must also be applied to the States through the Due Process Clause of the Fourteenth Amendment.

Justice Samuel Alito, writing for the majority, stated that the right to bear arms is a "fundamental right deeply rooted in the nation's history" and tradition. The Court's decision did not immediately overturn Chicago's handgun ban, but did establish a crucial precedent, extending Second Amendment protections to state and local levels. The NRA supported the plaintiffs in this case, viewing the ruling as further solidifying the right to bear arms across all levels of government and significantly limiting the ability of state and local jurisdictions to enact any restrictive gun control measures.

The NRA's Lobbying and Political Strategies

The NRA continues to exert considerable influence on gun policy through its extensive lobbying at both the federal and state levels, primarily conducted through its Institute for Legislative Action (NRA-ILA).Since 1975, the NRA-ILA has served as the organization's lobbying arm, dedicated to preserving the right of "law-abiding individuals to purchase, possess, and use firearms" for legitimate purposes, as guaranteed by the Second Amendment. The NRA-ILA actively engages in influencing legislation by directly interacting with lawmakers, bringing lawsuits related to gun rights, and endorsing or opposing political candidates based on their stances on firearm issues.

One notable example of the NRA's successful lobbying efforts was its role in the Firearm Owners Protection Act of 1986, which eased some of the restrictions imposed by the Gun Control Act of 1968. This was instrumental in the NRA's long-term goal of rolling back federal regulations. Another significant example of the NRA's influence was the Dickey Amendment, passed in 1996, which restricted the Centers for Disease Control and Prevention (CDC) from using federal funds to advocate for gun control, effectively stifling much-needed research on gun violence for many years. Data from OpenSecrets indicates that the NRA has spent millions of dollars on lobbying efforts over the years, demonstrating its financial commitment to influencing policy outcomes. This sustained and well-funded lobbying operation is a critical element of the NRA's strategy to shape gun policy in the United States.

The NRA plays a significant role in political campaigns through its Political Victory Fund (NRA-PVF), a political action committee (PAC) that publicly ranks political candidates and contributes financially to those who adequately support the NRA's pro-gun rights agenda. The NRA-PVF evaluates candidates, regardless of party affiliation, based on their voting records, public statements, and responses to NRA questionnaires, assigning them grades that can significantly impact their electability. The organization's endorsement and financial support can be vital for candidates in both primary and general elections. In the 2016 presidential election, the NRA spent *more than any other special interest group*, with approximately $30 million going to support Donald Trump's candidacy. This $30 million is separate from the additional millions dedicated to support Republican candidates in Senate races across the country. The NRA's influence in campaign finance extends beyond direct contributions, as its endorsements can sway voters, particularly those for whom gun rights are a primary concern. This active involvement in campaign finance and political spending underscores the NRA's commitment to electing officials who will support its legislative goals and oppose gun control measures at any cost.

    A key component of the NRA's political power lies in its ability to mobilize its large membership to engage in grassroots activism. With nearly five million members (though membership has been decreasing since its peak in 2012), the NRA can rally its base to contact lawmakers, participate in political campaigns, and advocate for or against specific gun policy proposals. The NRA uses this network and communication channels, including its website and publications like *America's 1st Freedom*, to inform members about legislative developments, encourage them to contact their elected officials, and organize efforts at the local, state, and federal levels. This ability to generate constituent pressure on policymakers is a significant asset in the NRA's lobbying efforts.

Many elected officials are highly responsive to the concerns of well-organized and vocal groups within their constituencies, and the NRA's membership provides a potent force in this regard. The dedication of its members, who often prioritize gun rights over all other issues in their voting decisions, further amplifies the NRA's political influence. This grassroots mobilization capacity allows the NRA to pressure lawmakers beyond direct lobbying and campaign contributions, making it a formidable voice in shaping the gun policy debate.

The NRA's Stance on Contemporary Gun Policy Issues

The NRA has consistently opposed the implementation of universal background checks on all firearm sales, arguing that such measures unfairly burden law-abiding citizens and fail to deter criminals, who will obtain firearms through illegal channels. While federal law requires licensed firearm dealers to conduct background checks through the National Instant Criminal Background Check System (NICS), the NRA resists efforts to expand this requirement to private gun sales, often referred to as the "gun show loophole" or "private sale loophole". The NRA insists that criminals do not obey gun laws and would not subject themselves to background checks when acquiring firearms illegally. The organization further argues that expanded background checks would inconvenience responsible gun owners without effectively preventing gun violence. It is worth noting, however, that despite the NRA's official stance, data indicates that most individual NRA members do support universal background checks, suggesting a potential disconnect between leadership's position and the views of its membership.

The NRA is a reliable opponent of bans on semi-automatic rifles, often labeled as "assault weapons," and restrictions on high-capacity magazines. They argue that the term "assault weapon" is a politically motivated mischaracterization of commonly owned firearms used for lawful purposes, including self-defense, hunting, and sport shooting. The NRA emphasizes that rifles, including semi-automatic rifles like the AR-15, are responsible for a relatively small fraction of violent crime compared to handguns.

Moreover, the NRA contends that bans on these types of firearms and magazines do not effectively reduce overall crime rates or prevent mass shootings. The organization points to studies suggesting that the Federal Assault Weapons Ban of 1994, which expired in 2004, had no significant impact on crime. The NRA views efforts to ban these firearms and magazines as an infringement on the Second Amendment rights of law-abiding citizens and a distraction from addressing the root causes of violence.

As previously discussed, the NRA's approach to reducing gun violence in schools centers on enhancing security measures and empowering trained individuals to respond to threats. The organization advocates for the presence of armed security personnel in schools and has, at times, supported the arming of trained teachers. The NRA consistently opposes gun control measures as a primary solution to school violence, arguing that such laws would not prevent determined attackers and would only disarm law-abiding citizens. Instead, the organization insists on addressing the ongoing epidemic of violence as strictly a mental health issue, ignoring the evidence that demonstrates otherwise. The NRA's stance reflects its belief that focusing on security and responsible gun handling is more effective than restricting access to firearms in preventing school shootings.

The NRA is a strong and consistent supporter of the Protection of Lawful Commerce in Arms Act (PLCAA), enacted in 2005. This federal law provides significant legal protection to firearms manufacturers, distributors, dealers, and importers from lawsuits resulting from the criminal misuse of their products by others. The NRA views the PLCAA as an essential safeguard for the firearms industry from what it considers to be frivolous and politically motivated lawsuits intended to bankrupt lawful businesses.

The organization argues that holding gun manufacturers and sellers liable for the actions of criminals is unfair and could lead to the demise of a "critical" industry. While the PLCAA includes some exceptions, such as cases involving defective products or negligent actions, the NRA opposes any efforts to repeal or weaken this legislation, seeing it as a crucial defense against the gun control lobby's attempts to undermine the Second Amendment through litigation.

The NRA's role in shaping gun policy in the United States cannot be overstated. Far from its original mission of teaching marksmanship to militia members, the NRA has evolved into a singularly powerful, and ideologically manipulative, political force with a clear and consistent agenda of opposing nearly any gun control legislation in the service of profit. This transformation has profoundly undercut the possibility of any intellectually honest national debate on firearms. The NRA has successfully derailed any legislative potential for gun control regulation and has reframed the judicial and public interpretations of the right to bear arms.

Chapter 5: The Complexities of Armed Security

The NRA and other supporters of unregulated and unchecked access to firearms would have us believe that only "a good guy with a gun can stop a bad guy with a gun." As we have seen, this simplistic view of a complex situation has created an environment where popular opinion and observable reality are at odds with each other. In some cases, the good guy with a gun either accidentally or intentionally becomes the bad guy, either while in service of a perceived good or due to extremist behavior in defense of Second Amendment rights.

In this chapter, we will explore the alarming rise in school shootings across the United States and assess the concurrent increase of armed security personnel on school campuses. It is important that we do not assume causation with correlation here. The sharp rise in school shootings since the 1970s, while dramatic, is outpaced in orders of magnitude by the increase in armed guards. If there was an effective measure of safety to be inferred from the presence of armed security, it should be demonstrated in the data. In truth, the data tells a very different story.

Here we will see a statistical overview of the trends, will analyze the efficacy and consequences of armed security, and look more closely at detailed case studies of four seminal school shootings: Columbine High School, Sandy Hook Elementary School, Marjory Stoneman Douglas High School, and Robb Elementary School. For each incident, I will attempt to summarize the event, detail the security measures in place at the time, and outline the lessons learned by law enforcement, school administration, security professionals, and behavioral health experts in the aftermath.

A significant reality is the dramatic escalation in the frequency and lethality of school shootings since 1970. While the presence of armed security, including School Resource Officers (SROs), has also markedly increased, research on their effectiveness in preventing or mitigating these tragedies is at best contradictory. Several studies indicate no definitive deterrent effect, and some analyses even suggest a correlation between armed guards and higher casualty rates in occurred incidents. Furthermore, the deployment of armed personnel is associated with significant unintended consequences, including negative impacts on school climate and disproportionately higher rates of disciplinary actions for minority students and students with disabilities.

(Deterrence, importantly, is the most often reason given by parents for their support of policies that include armed officers in schools. Though evidence cannot prove a negative, there is a notable lack of evidence suggesting any deterrence of violence based on security personnel or other hardening policies.)

The case studies we'll look at here reveal recurring failures in prevention, threat assessment, communication, and emergency response, even in schools with an armed presence. Columbine spurred a nationwide shift in law enforcement tactics from "contain and wait" to immediate engagement. Sandy Hook highlighted vulnerabilities in physical security and the profound need for mental health support, particularly for young victims. Parkland exposed the devastating consequences of an SRO's failure to act and systemic breakdowns in addressing clear warning signs. Uvalde underscored a catastrophic collapse of law enforcement command and adherence to established active shooter protocols, alongside critical failures in basic school security measures.

We must also address the significant behavioral health and educational impacts of active shooter and "code red" drills on students, particularly those in kindergarten and early elementary grades. Evidence indicates these drills, especially when unannounced or highly realistic, can induce anxiety, stress, depression, and trauma, potentially disrupting the learning environment and students' sense of safety.

As we will see, ensuring school safety requires a multi-layered, evidence-based approach that extends beyond a primary reliance on armed security. I argue that prioritizing comprehensive prevention strategies such as robust mental health services, effective threat assessment programs, and fostering positive school climates are critical to driving meaningful reform in safety awareness and culture. I call for a comprehensive re-evaluation of the role and scope of armed school security, with reforms to active shooter drill practices that ensure they are trauma-informed and age-appropriate. Continued investment in research, enhanced inter-agency collaboration, and addressing broader societal factors contributing to violence are also paramount.

The Enduring Challenge of School Shootings

School shootings represent one of the most distressing and persistent challenges facing American society. These acts of violence shatter the perceived sanctity of educational institutions, leaving indelible scars on students, educators, families, and entire communities. The United States, regrettably, holds the distinction of having the highest number of school-related shootings globally, a statistic that underscores the urgency and complexity of addressing this crisis. Each incident reignites national debates on gun control, mental health, and the fundamental right to safety in schools, and each movement ultimately fails to bring meaningful change.

The impact of school shootings extends far beyond the immediate casualties. They instill fear, disrupt learning, and can have long-lasting psychological consequences for survivors and those indirectly exposed. In response to this escalating threat, schools and policymakers have implemented a variety of safety measures, with a significant emphasis placed on increasing the presence of armed security personnel and conducting preparedness drills.

The Escalation of School Shootings in the United States

The landscape of school safety in the United States has been irrevocably altered by a significant and deeply concerning escalation in school shooting incidents. Statistical data compiled over recent decades paints a somewhat counterintuitive picture of the increasing frequency, fatalities, and widespread impact on student populations.

Trends in Frequency, Fatalities, and Victim Demographics

A comprehensive study analyzing data from the Center for Homeland Defense and Security (CHDS) through May 2022 revealed a dramatic rise in school shootings over a 53-year period. The annual number of incidents surged from 20 in 1970 to a peak of 251 in 2021, representing a more than twelve-fold increase. This surge has had a direct and devastating impact on children; the likelihood of a child becoming a school shooting victim has increased by more than 400 percent since 1970, and the rate of death from such incidents has risen by more than 600 percent. Specifically, the rate of children being school shooting victims escalated from 0.49 per 1 million population in 1970 to 2.21 per 1 million in 2021, while the death rate for children increased from 0.16 to 0.97 per 1 million population during the same timeframe. The study analyzed a total of 2,056 school shooting incidents involving 3,083 victims, of whom 2,033 were aged 5-17. The study also included 1,050 adults aged 18-74, representing school staff, parents, and others present during the events.

Regional disparities are also evident. While states like California (214 incidents), Texas (176), and Florida (120) recorded the highest absolute numbers of school shootings in the period studied, the District of Columbia (5.5 per 100 schools), Delaware (5.4), and Louisiana (4.6) exhibited the highest rates of school shootings when normalized per 100 schools. More recent tracking by Education Week further highlights this disturbing trend, documenting 228 school shootings that resulted in injuries or deaths between 2018 and early May 2025, with a notable increase in 2021 through 2024 compared to the early 2000s.

Weaponry and Shooter Characteristics

The types of weapons used in school shootings vary, but handguns are by far the most common, accounting for 84 percent of incidents. Rifles (including the AR-15) were used in 7 percent of incidents and shotguns in 4 percent. Despite their less frequent use, rifles have proven to be the deadliest, as the rifle is a weapon designed for killing (hunting or military) and the handgun is primarily a defensive weapon.

Victims and shooters are predominantly male, accounting for 77 percent of victims and 96 percent of shooters. A significant and concerning finding is the age of the perpetrators: nearly two-thirds of shooters were under the age of 17. Early profiling efforts by the Federal Bureau of Investigation (FBI) described shooters as often being "middle-class, lonely or alienated, awkward, Caucasian males who had access to firearms." Access to firearms is a critical factor, with data indicating that 68 percent of shooters obtain weapons from their own home or the home of a relative. Since 1999, in school shootings committed by children or adolescents, 80 percent of the guns used were taken from their homes or a relative's home.

The motivations behind these acts are complex and varied. Studies suggest common motives include experiences of bullying, persecution, or being threatened (reported by 75 percent of attackers), a desire for revenge (61 percent), an attempt to solve a problem (34 percent), suicidal ideation or depression (27 percent), and seeking attention or recognition (24 percent). The prevalence of these factors, particularly the high percentage of shooters obtaining weapons from home environments and the young age of many perpetrators, points towards a multifaceted problem that extends beyond the immediate school environment. It suggests that effective prevention strategies must address broader societal issues, including responsible firearm storage, youth mental health services, and the underlying causes of alienation and grievance among young people.

Databases and Data Sources

Understanding the scope and nature of school shootings relies on comprehensive data collection. The K-12 School Shooting Database (K-12 SSDB) is a significant national resource that documents every instance a gun is fired, brandished with intent to harm, or a bullet hits school property, regardless of the number of victims, time of day, or reason. Its methodology includes detailed information for each school shooting, a reliability score quantifying the dependability of the information, and verified primary source citations to facilitate further academic research. Other vital data sources include the National Center for Education Statistics (NCES) and the Bureau of Justice Statistics (BJS), which provide broader data on school crime and safety.

The accelerating frequency of school shootings, coupled with the characteristics of the perpetrators and their access to firearms, underscores the complexity of this issue. It suggests that while school-based security measures are part of the conversation, a comprehensive solution must also address factors rooted in homes, communities, and broader societal dynamics concerning mental health and firearm accessibility.

Armed Security on Campus: Trends, Debates, and Efficacy

In response to the escalating crisis of school shootings, a prominent strategy adopted by educational institutions and policymakers across the United States has been the increased deployment of armed security personnel on school campuses. This section examines the statistical trends in this deployment, delves into the ongoing debate surrounding its effectiveness as a deterrent, and reviews the evidence regarding its impact on school safety and the broader school environment.

The Rise of Armed Presence in U.S. Schools

Data from various sources indicate a significant increase in the presence of armed security in U.S. public schools over the past decade and a half, although some recent figures suggest a potential plateau or slight decline.

According to a Pew Research Center analysis, in the 2019-20 school year, 65 percent of public K-12 schools reported having at least one security staff person present at the school at least once a week (this same figure in 1970 was approximately 1 percent). This marked a substantial rise from 43 percent in the 2009-10 school year. More specifically, the presence of sworn law enforcement officers (often School Resource Officers, or SROs) who routinely carried a firearm on campus increased from 28 percent of public schools in 2009-10 to 51 percent in 2019-20.

The National Center for Education Statistics (NCES) data aligns with this upward trend through 2019-20. However, more recent NCES data for the 2021-22 school year, as reported by some outlets, indicated a decrease, with 45 percent of public schools having a sworn law enforcement officer routinely carrying a firearm. Another source analyzing NCES data for 2021-22 reported that 46 percent of public schools employed SROs, and 25 percent were staffed with a sworn law enforcement officer who routinely carried a firearm, a notable drop from the 51 percent figure in 2019-20. This discrepancy between the longer-term trend and the most recent figures warrants careful consideration, potentially reflecting pandemic-related shifts, changes in funding priorities, or variations in data collection and reporting methodologies.

The presence of armed security is not uniform across all schools. Larger schools and secondary schools (middle and high schools) are significantly more likely to have security staff and armed officers compared to smaller schools and elementary schools. For instance, in 2019-20, 96 percent of schools with 1,000 or more students had security staff, compared to 48 percent of schools with fewer than 300 students. Similarly, over 80 percent of middle and high schools had security staff, versus 55 percent of elementary schools. An important demographic disparity also exists; schools where more than three-quarters of the students are racial or ethnic minorities are less likely to have an officer who carries a firearm (43 percent) compared to schools where a quarter or fewer students are minorities (57 percent). The question that arises here is, "if armed security is effective in protecting kids, which kids are more likely to receive that protection?" (Hint: it's not the minority populations.)

Does Armed Security Prevent or Mitigate School Shootings?

The fundamental argument favoring armed security in schools is rooted in the concept of deterrence and rapid response—the NRA's popular "good guys with guns" hypothesis. Proponents contend that an armed presence can discourage potential attackers and, should an attack occur, enable a faster, more effective intervention to neutralize the threat and minimize casualties. Some also argue that arming school staff is a more cost-effective measure than hiring dedicated security officers. The Federal Commission on School Safety, for instance, suggested that SROs are "best positioned to respond to acts of violence".

However, a substantial body of research and expert analysis challenges these assertions, presenting a far more complex and often contradictory picture of the efficacy of armed school security.

Numerous studies and reviews conclude that there is little to no definitive empirical evidence that the presence of SROs or other armed guards prevents school shootings or significantly mitigates their severity. A 2021 study by researchers at the University at Albany, using national school-level data, found that while SROs may reduce some forms of non-firearm school violence, they do not prevent school shootings or gun-related incidents. The study even suggested that SRO presence might marginally increase the likelihood of a school shooting, potentially due to increased detection and reporting of firearm offenses.

Counterintuitively, some research indicates that the presence of armed guards may be associated with worse outcomes in school shootings. A study by The Violence Project, analyzing data from the K-12 School Shooting Database for incidents between 1980 and 2019, found that shootings at schools with an armed guard present resulted in, on average, three times as many people killed. Similarly, a dissertation from Prairie View A&M University, also utilizing the K-12 SSDB, identified a statistically significant association between SRO presence and a higher number of casualties in school shooting incidents. Researchers theorize that because many school shooters are suicidal, an armed officer might act as an incentive rather than a deterrent, or that the presence of additional firearms can escalate the violence.

The argument for armed security is significantly undermined by its failure in several high-profile school shootings. At Columbine High School, an armed SRO was on campus but did not neutralize the attackers. At Marjory Stoneman Douglas High School, the assigned SRO infamously remained outside the building during the massacre. At Robb Elementary School in Uvalde, hundreds of heavily armed law enforcement officers, including school district police, were present but failed to engage the shooter for over an hour. These incidents demonstrate that the mere presence of armed personnel does not guarantee an effective response or prevention.

Instances where an armed guard or SRO has successfully intervened to stop a school shooting are rare, with only a handful of such cases being well-documented. Perhaps shockingly, data suggests that more security officers have been identified as perpetrators of school violence than those who have been credited with stopping a violent rampage.

Beyond the debate over direct efficacy in active shooter events, the presence of armed security in schools is linked to several significant negative consequences suggesting that heightened policing and intrusive security measures can decrease students' sense of safety and contribute to a more punitive school environment.

A consistent finding across multiple studies is that SRO presence is strongly associated with increased rates of student suspensions, expulsions, police referrals, and arrests, particularly for minor offenses. These disciplinary actions disproportionately affect students of color (especially Black students), male students, and students with disabilities, contributing to the "school-to-prison pipeline".

The substantial financial investment required for armed personnel raises serious questions about resource allocation, as these funds could potentially be directed towards other, more effective safety strategies, such as mental health services, counseling, and programs aimed at improving school climate—approaches that I argue is far more foundational to violence prevention.

It is also important to note the increased risk of accidental shootings, misuse of firearms in moments of passion, or racially biased (whether implicit or explicit) use of force if more personnel are armed within schools.

The evidence suggests a significant disconnect between the intuitive appeal of placing armed defenders in schools and the empirical reality of their impact. While the desire for immediate, visible action in the face of horrific violence is understandable, the data indicates that armed security is not a straightforward solution and carries with it a complex array of potential harm and limited proven benefits in preventing the most catastrophic events. This points to the necessity of a more nuanced, evidence-based discussion about the role of armed personnel within a broader, multi-layered school safety strategy, rather than viewing them as a standalone panacea. The decision to increase armed presence in schools involves weighing these often-unproven benefits against known and significant negative consequences for the educational environment and student equity.

Chapter 6: Case Studies from Major School Shootings

The current direction taken in school safety policy and practice in the United States has been understandably shaped by a series of high-profile mass shootings. Examining these events—Columbine, Sandy Hook, Parkland, and Uvalde—offers important insights into the evolution of threats, the efficacy of security measures, the performance of armed personnel, and the multifaceted lessons learned across law enforcement, school administration, security, and behavioral health domains.

I will not attempt to assert any special knowledge or expertise in these cases. My reviews and summaries of each event presented are based on reporting and data made publicly available by those who were present or other subject matter experts, including law enforcement. Much has been written and reported about each of these horrible attacks, and I do not want to relitigate any of them or reopen any associated trauma, so I will not attempt to present the full narrative of each attack. Rather, I will focus on what we have learned about school safety in the aftermath and try to understand if those lessons are serving us well or if we should find new paths to understanding.

I will not use the names of perpetrators, to not offer any additional celebrity to their status. I will do my best to honor the victims.

Columbine High School (1999)

On April 20, 1999, two senior students followed through with a planned attack on Columbine High School in Littleton, Colorado. They killed 12 of their fellow students and one teacher, while injuring 23 others before taking their own lives in the school's library. They initially planned on detonating two large propane bombs in the cafeteria that would have potentially kill hundreds more. They had hoped to drive survivors of the explosion into their gunfire outside. Their makeshift bombs failed to explode, however, and the subsequent shooting spree appeared to target victims randomly, contrary to initial speculation.

School security at Columbine in April 1999 was minimal by today's standards. The school employed "a handful of cameras outside the school and a few school resource officers." An armed Jefferson County Sheriff's Deputy was assigned as the full-time SRO and was on campus, reportedly eating lunch in his patrol car at the west end of the student parking lot when the attack began near the cafeteria entrance. There was no comprehensive, district-wide incident command structure in place, and local law enforcement agencies had limited familiarity with the school's complex interior layout. Lockdown drills were not common practice.

The SRO was one of the first to respond upon hearing the shots. He exchanged gunfire with one shooter outside the school but was unable to neutralize him. The predominant law enforcement tactic at the time was to establish a perimeter, contain the situation, and wait for specialized SWAT teams to arrive and make entry. This approach led to significant delays in law enforcement entering the school and reaching victims. It took hours for officers to secure the building, during which time some victims, including Dave Sanders, a teacher and coach, bled to death while awaiting medical attention.

Lessons Learned

The most profound lesson from Columbine was the critical need to overhaul active shooter response tactics. The "contain and wait" strategy was inarguably a catastrophic failure, directly contributing to the body count. This failure led to the widespread adoption of the Immediate Action Rapid Deployment (IARD) protocol, which trains the first responding officers, even a single officer, to move directly toward the sound of gunfire to neutralize the shooter and stop the killing. The incident also highlighted the necessity for improved interagency communication, better officer training in active shooter scenarios for all patrol officers, not just SWAT, and familiarity with school layouts.

Columbine forced a fundamental shift in how schools viewed threats, moving from a primary focus on external dangers to recognizing the potential for violence from within the student body. This realization necessitated the development and implementation of school-based threat assessment teams, designed to identify, evaluate, and intervene with students exhibiting warning signs of potential violence. The shooters demonstrated several of these signs, including violent writings, online posts, and discussions about weapons, which were not effectively pieced together or acted upon. Clear, practiced emergency protocols, including lockdown procedures (which were vanishingly rare prior to 1999), were deemed.

Locked classroom doors, where teachers were able to quickly understand the threat and react, proved to be lifesaving. Physical security enhancements, including single point controlled entry, classroom doors that lock from the inside, and increased use of security cameras, became more common in schools post-Columbine. Improved information sharing among school staff, administrators, and law enforcement was also identified as crucial, as was the need for comprehensive crisis communication planning.

The tragedy underscored the profound and widespread psychological trauma inflicted on students, staff, survivors, and the broader community. It highlighted the critical need for immediate and sustained mental health support, including crisis counseling, trauma-informed care, and resources to address conditions like PTSD, anxiety, and survivor's guilt. The importance of peer support networks and the need to foster a sense of community in the aftermath were also recognized.

While the shooters' specific motivations remain unconfirmed, their mental health challenges (one was reportedly on a prescription antidepressant, the other was diagnosed with depression) contributed to a greater, and still evolving, awareness of youth behavioral health issues and the need for accessible support systems. The narrative that the shooters were primarily motivated by bullying was largely refuted by investigations, which pointed to more complex psychological issues and a desire for infamy.

Columbine was clearly a watershed event. It fundamentally changed the popular understanding of school violence in America. It exposed critical deficiencies in both law enforcement tactics and school preparedness for internal threats. While it tragically served as a dark inspiration for subsequent attackers, it also drove significant, nationwide changes in active shooter response protocols, the implementation of threat assessment models, and an increased focus on the physical security of school buildings.

    However, the challenge of effectively identifying and intervening with deeply troubled youth before they resort to violence, and balancing enhanced security with a supportive school climate, remains a central and ongoing struggle.

Sandy Hook Elementary School (2012)

On December 14, 2012, a 20-year-old shot his mother and then drove to Sandy Hook Elementary School in Newtown, Connecticut. He was armed with a rifle and multiple handguns, all legally purchased by his mother. He proceeded to shoot his way through the school's locked glass entrance panel, and less than 12 minutes later he had murdered 20 first-graders and six adult staff members before killing himself before law enforcement officers were able to engage with him.

Sandy Hook Elementary had recently upgraded its security protocols, including a system where visitors had to be individually buzzed in after a visual and identification review via a video monitor at the front entrance. The school doors were locked each day at 9:30 a.m. after student arrivals. The shooter got through the primary security layer by shooting through the thick glass panel adjacent to the locked front doors, and his first victims were administrators and support staff.

Critically, while the main entrance was secured, individual classroom doors were not uniformly locked. The final investigative report indicated that the two classrooms where the victims were killed had unlocked doors and showed no signs of forced entry, suggesting the shooter gained immediate access once inside the building.

No armed security personnel were present on the school campus at the time of the attack, but relatively prompt arrival of Newtown police officers and Connecticut State Police is cited as likely prompting the shooter to commit suicide, ending the rampage and preventing further casualties.

Lessons Learned

The rapid response by law enforcement, though unable to prevent the initial massacre, was recognized as critical in halting the shooter's actions, reinforcing the importance of the post-Columbine IARD tactics. The incident also highlighted the need for diversified emergency drills that account for scenarios where school leadership might be incapacitated early in an event, as the principal and school psychologist were among the first victims. Reliable and redundant communication systems for first responders remained a key concern.

The heroism of school staff, many of whom sacrificed their lives to protect students, was widely recognized in reporting. The actions of staff who implemented lockdown procedures quickly, and the custodian who ran through the halls alerting others undoubtedly saved lives, proving that trained and empowered personnel are a crucial first line of defense.

Classroom door security has become a focal point of security planning. The fact that the shooter entered unlocked classrooms led to a nationwide push for all classroom doors to be quickly lockable from the inside, and to be kept locked during instructional time. The shooter's method of breaching the main entrance by shooting through glass also spurred widespread adoption of reinforced or ballistic-resistant glass in school entryways and vulnerable areas. This is part a practice now known as "hardening" the school against violent attacks.

The tragedy brought about significant changes in school security best practices, including recommendations for single, controlled points of entry with secured vestibules, direct video surveillance feeds from schools to police dispatch, and the use of police radios within schools for faster communication.

Comprehensive emergency operations plans now will typically include detailed protocols for lockdowns, evacuations, parent-student reunification, crisis communications, and integrated mental health support. "Safe and Sound: A Sandy Hook Initiative" was developed by parents of victims, promoting an "Assess, Act, and Audit" model for school safety.

The extreme youth of the victims at Sandy Hook brought the psychological impact of such violence on children into sharp focus, highlighting the need for developmentally appropriate trauma information and long-term mental health care for survivors, families, and the community. The importance of self-care for responders and community members, establishing trust, and utilizing therapeutic communication in the recovery process were underscored.

The shooter's history included diagnosis of autism spectrum disorder, depression, anxiety, and obsessive-compulsive disorder, along with an "atypical preoccupation with violence." Most importantly, he had easy access to his mother's firearms. While a Connecticut State Attorney's report concluded these factors "neither caused nor led to his murderous acts," the case intensified national discussions about youth mental health identification and support systems, parental responsibility in securing firearms, and the potential need for mechanisms like Extreme Risk Protection Orders (ERPOs), or "red flag" laws. Organizations like The Sandy Hook Promise were founded in part to advocate for gun safety reforms and to promote mental health wellness programs like "Know the Signs" to prevent violence.

The profound tragedy of Sandy Hook, particularly the targeting of very young children in what would was popularly understood to be a safe suburban elementary school, served as a powerful catalyst for change. (The racial bias implicit in this assumption is noted.) It led to a significant focus on "hardening" school facilities through enhanced physical security measures, especially concerning entry points and classroom door integrity. Simultaneously, it amplified calls for improved mental health services for youth and stricter gun control measures, although legislative outcomes on the latter remained contentious. The event reinforced the critical importance of rapid law enforcement response but also laid bare the devastating reality that even a few minutes of unimpeded access by an attacker inside a school can lead to catastrophic loss of life.

Marjory Stoneman Douglas High School (2018)

On February 14, 2018, a previously expelled 19-year-old former student opened fire at Marjory Stoneman Douglas (MSD) High School in Parkland, Florida. Armed with an AR-15 style rifle, he killed 14 students and 3 staff members and injured 17 others in an attack that lasted approximately six minutes. The shooter was arrested later that day.

MSD employed an armed sheriff's deputy, as its School Resource Officer (SRO). He was on campus during the attack. The school also utilized a campus monitor system. However, policies regarding the initiation of a "Code Red" lockdown were reportedly unclear; staff had been trained not to call a lockdown unless they directly saw a weapon or heard gunshots, a *reactive* rather than *proactive* stance.

Furthermore, many classrooms within the freshman building, where most of the attack occurred, lacked clearly designated "hard corners" or safe hiding areas, and access to some potential safe spaces was obstructed by furniture. The Broward County School District had also previously implemented lenient disciplinary policies, sometimes referred to as "restorative justice" approaches. (Note: the "restorative justice" practices identified here are not representative of the practices outlined elsewhere is this book.) Critics argue these policies failed to adequately address the shooter's previous extensive history of behavioral problems, threats, and warning signs prior to his expulsion.

The assigned SRO remained outside during the entirety of the shooting, never entering or attempting to engage the shooter. His actions (or lack thereof) became a central point of criticism and investigation. He was later arrested and charged with child neglect and perjury, though he was ultimately found not guilty of the criminal charges. Other deputies who arrived on scene also did not immediately enter the building. Officers from the neighboring Coral Springs Police Department were among the first law enforcement personnel to enter the building and begin rendering aid.

Lessons Learned

The failure of the SRO to adhere to active shooter protocol—which dictates immediate engagement of the threat—was a catastrophic lapse that drew widespread condemnation and scrutiny. This incident raised profound questions about the training, preparedness, and disposition of armed personnel in schools. It underscored the critical need for clear incident command structures, robust interagency coordination, and joint training exercises between different law enforcement agencies and other first responders.

The positive example of Coral Springs Police Department's coordination with their Fire Department, based on prior joint training, was noted by several reports. Ensuring all responding officers are adequately equipped with long guns, breaching tools, and bleeding control kits, and are proficient in their use, was also emphasized. A significant lesson was the imperative for law enforcement to study and adapt to the evolving tactics of mass shooters, who often learn from previous incidents.

The Parkland tragedy highlighted glaring deficiencies in school-level preparedness and response. A primary lesson was the need for clear, unambiguous policies allowing *any* school employee to initiate a lockdown or "Code Red" and the necessity for effective, campus-wide alert systems, such as panic buttons (leading to "Alyssa's Law" in Florida and other states). Physical security enhancements became a renewed focus, including single points of entry, classroom doors that lock automatically or from the inside, as well as perimeter fencing, security gates, and the designation and clearing of "hard corners" or safer spaces within classrooms. Upgraded surveillance cameras systems accessible in real-time by law enforcement were also recommended.

The critical importance of a robust threat assessment program as part of a larger culture where all warning signs are taken seriously and reported was made plain. In Parkland, the shooter had a well-documented history of disturbing behavior, threats of violence, and mental health concerns that were not adequately addressed or communicated between relevant agencies. Failures in the school's disciplinary system and information sharing were also identified as significant contributing factors.

In response to the shooting, Florida passed the Marjory Stoneman Douglas High School Public Safety Act, which mandated sweeping changes including the provision for armed "Guardians" on every school campus (in addition to SROs), increased funding for school mental health services, the establishment of "red flag" laws (ERPOs), and raising the minimum age to purchase firearms from 18 to 21.

The shooting amplified the national conversation about youth mental health and the need for early identification and intervention for at-risk students. Understanding the "pathway to violence"—often involving grievances, violent ideation, and planning—became a key focus for violence prevention efforts. The importance of accessible and effective anonymous reporting systems (like Florida's FortifyFL app) and strategies to overcome the bystander effect in reporting concerning behaviors were emphasized. The immense trauma experienced by the survivors, many of whom became vocal advocates for change, highlighted the long-term mental health consequences and the need for comprehensive support systems.

Parkland served as a grim illustration that the mere presence of an armed SRO is insufficient if that individual is not adequately trained, prepared, or willing to follow established protocols and engage a threat. The incident exposed deep systemic failures in school discipline, threat assessment processes, and inter-agency communication, occurring despite years of lessons purportedly learned from prior school shootings. The powerful student-led activism that emerged from Parkland significantly shaped subsequent policy debates and legislative action nationwide, driving changes that aimed to both "harden" schools and address mental health and gun access issues. However, the push for more armed personnel, such as the Guardian program, in the wake of an SRO's failure, highlights the persistent incongruities in school safety approaches.

Robb Elementary School (2022)

Most recently of the examples presented here, and with echoes of Sandy Hook, was the shooting in Uvalde, Texas. On May 24, 2022, an 18-year-old former student of the Uvalde Consolidated Independent School District (UCISD), shot his grandmother at their residence before driving to Robb Elementary School. As in so many other rampages, the shooter came armed with an AR-15 style rifle, entered the school, and fatally shot 19 fourth-grade students and two teachers. He injured 17 others before finally being confronted and killed by law enforcement officers.

The Uvalde Consolidated Independent School District (UCISD) had its own six-officer police department and had reportedly more than doubled its security budget in the four years leading up to the shooting. Security measures in place across the district included social media monitoring software (Social Sentinel), a visitor management system (Raptor), two-way radios for staff, perimeter fencing around campuses, school-based threat-assessment teams, and an official policy requiring classroom doors to be locked.

However, failures in the implementation of these measures at Robb Elementary were later identified. A Texas House of Representatives investigative report found that exterior and classroom doors were often left unlocked or propped open, partly due to a "shortage of keys" and a "culture of complacency" regarding security alerts, as many were false alarms related to border patrol activities. The shooter entered the school through an unlocked door; this door could only be locked from the *outside*, a glaring security flaw.

An armed UCISD police officer was reportedly at the school but, as is so often the case, did not immediately engage the shooter upon his arrival. Ultimately, nearly 400 law enforcement officers from local, state, and federal agencies converged on Robb Elementary. Despite this overwhelming armed presence, there was an approximate 75-minute delay from the time the first officers arrived on scene to when a tactical team finally breached the classroom and neutralized the shooter. During this period, children and teachers remained trapped with the active shooter, making desperate 911 calls.

Lessons Learned

The response was characterized by the DOJ as a series of "cascading failures." The most significant failure was arguably the decision by law enforcement on scene to treat the incident as a "barricaded suspect" situation rather than an active shooter event, thereby violating established protocol that mandates immediate engagement to stop the killing. Officers failed to prioritize saving innocent lives over their own safety.

There was no clear, effective on-scene leadership or established Incident Command System (ICS), leading to chaos, conflicting orders, and a lack of coordinated action among the multitude of responding agencies.

Severe communication problems plagued the response, including issues with radio interoperability, lack of clear information dissemination, and conflicting messages to officers and the public. This extended to misinformation provided to victims' families, causing additional lingering trauma.

The DOJ report and other investigations highlighted critical failures in even the most basic door security. The fact that the shooter entered through an unlocked exterior door and that classroom doors were not consistently locked (and in some cases, had malfunctioning locks or locks that required a key from the hallway side) were major contributing factors to the tragedy. One important takeaway should be to ensure all doors are functional, consistently locked per policy, and that classroom doors can be quickly secured from the inside.

The school's reliance on a traditional single-option lockdown was obviously insufficient and may have contributed to the overall loss of life. Staff and students reportedly ran back into the building to lock down instead of evacuating when the shooting began outside. Recommendations by the DOJ included adopting multi-option response training (evacuation, enhanced lockdown, engage/barricade) and training students to evacuate even without direct adult supervision.

While the school used its Raptor notification system, issues with cell service and internet access meant some alerts were not received. This points to the need for redundant and reliable internal and external communication systems. Effective dispatcher training is also critical. Reports indicated that emergency dispatchers reportedly told children in direct contact with the gunman to remain quiet rather than evacuation if feasible.

Inaccurate or outdated interior school maps and lack of readily available master keys for law enforcement also hindered the response. Key boxes and up-to-date digital blueprints accessible to responders have since been recommended as part of the safety plan.

The Uvalde shooter, as in other events, had a troubled background, including being deemed "at risk" by the school system in fourth grade, but reportedly never received consistent special education services or mental health support. He exhibited numerous warning signs, including self-harm, animal cruelty, and troubling social media posts indicating an intent to commit violence, which were largely ignored. This again shows the persistent gaps in cohesion between threat assessment pathways and mental health intervention systems.

The aftermath required extensive, victim-centered, culturally sensitive, and linguistically appropriate trauma support services for the students, families, staff, and the wider Uvalde community. The DOJ report stressed the importance of coordinating mental health professionals and properly vetting service providers to avoid overwhelming or inadequately serving the affected population.

The Robb Elementary shooting stands as a catastrophic failure of the law enforcement response, demonstrating that an overwhelming armed presence is ineffective without decisive leadership, clear communication, adherence to established active shooter protocols, and basic operational competence.

It also served as a stark reminder that fundamental physical security measures, such as ensuring doors are consistently locked and functional, are critical and can be fatally undermined by human factors and systemic neglect. The event reiterated the urgent need for robust systems to identify and support at-risk individuals and to ensure that warning signs of potential violence are effectively communicated and acted upon.

The immense and prolonged suffering of the Uvalde community underscored the critical importance of a well-coordinated, culturally competent, and sustained behavioral health response following such devastating trauma.

Chapter 7: Active Shooter Drills and Well-being

In an effort to prepare for the unthinkable, schools across the United States have widely adopted active shooter drills, often referred to as "lockdown" or "code red" drills. In the 2019-20 school year, 98 percent of public schools reported having written procedures for active shooter situations, and 96 percent had conducted lockdown drills with students that year. By the 2023-24 school year, 98 percent of public schools reported having written procedures for active shooter drills. While intended to enhance safety and preparedness, a growing body of research and expert opinion raises serious concerns about the behavioral health and educational consequences of these drills, particularly for our youngest students.

Consequences for Young Students (K - 5)

The psychological toll of active shooter drills on young children can be significant, manifesting as increased anxiety, stress, depression, and even trauma.

Multiple studies have documented the correlation between active shooter drills and heightened negative emotional states in students. A notable 2021 study analyzed social media data, finding that active shooter drills were associated with a 42 percent increase in stress and anxiety, a 39 percent increase in depression, and a 23 percent increase in physiological health problems in children as young as five years old, as well as their parents and teachers. Concerns over death also saw a 22 percent increase in related online discussions within communities following a drill.

Young children in kindergarten through third grade are particularly vulnerable, often experiencing confusion due to their developmental stage, struggling to separate the abstract nature of the threat or to differentiate a drill from a real event, especially when stressed or anxious. This can lead to increased and ongoing separation anxiety, somatic complaints like headaches or stomachaches, and behavioral regressions including thumb sucking or a reliance on diapers. Anecdotal evidence, such as a kindergartner requiring a year of therapy for extreme anxiety after being alone in a bathroom during a drill, underscores the potential for severe distress. At an incident in my own town, students were isolated in unlocked bathrooms and forced to stand on toilets for hours while a reported event was cleared.

Active shooter drills, especially those that are unannounced or involve highly realistic simulations (using simulated gunfire, injuries, or actors), can trigger past trauma or induce new trauma in students. The American Academy of Pediatrics and other expert bodies have cautioned against such high-intensity drills.

Repeated exposure to fear-inducing drills may have complex long-term effects. Some students may become desensitized to the perceived threat of violence, potentially under-responding in an actual emergency. Conversely, for others, these drills can cultivate a persistent state of fear and hypervigilance, eroding their sense of safety at school. The human brain's threat-detection system can be mistakenly activated by realistic drills, leading to prolonged fight-or-flight responses that are unhealthy for children's developing brains.

Educational Impacts

The psychological distress caused by active shooter drills can also have tangible impacts on the educational environment and student outcomes.

Active shooter drills consume already strictly outlined instructional time. Beyond the time taken for the drill itself, the heightened anxiety and fear experienced by some students can make it difficult for them to concentrate, engage in learning, and process information effectively once classroom activities resume, sometimes for days after the drill. Some educators and mental health professionals worry that frequent, intense drills can contribute to a "prison-like" atmosphere in schools, fundamentally shifting them from nurturing learning environments to places perceived as primarily focused on security and danger, where students are primarily seen as threats, not learners.

There is evidence linking feelings of unsafety to school avoidance, truancy, and dropout rates. For example, the Youth Risk Behavior Survey indicated that 13 percent of high school students reported not going to school at least once in the past 30 days because they felt unsafe. While not solely attributable to drills, a climate of fear, potentially exacerbated by drills, can contribute to such feelings.

Some studies suggest that instead of reassuring students, certain types of drills may diminish their perception of school safety. An Urban Institute study analyzing data from Arkansas found slightly lower attendance rates in academic quarters when active-shooter drills occurred. The same study also found that elementary students (grades 3-5) who took standardized tests on school days immediately following an active-shooter drill had lower proficiency rates in English and math, though these rates returned to typical levels in subsequent weeks. This suggests a temporary negative impact on academic performance, potentially due to emotional distress or reduced instructional time for test preparation.

Chapter 8: Legislation for Comprehensive Safety

Public policy at the state and federal levels plays a crucial role in shaping the landscape of school safety. Legislation can either reinforce outdated, punitive models or pave the way for more comprehensive, supportive, and evidence-based approaches. Crafting policies that genuinely foster holistic school safety requires a nuanced understanding of what works, a commitment to equity, and a focus on providing schools with the resources and support they need for effective implementation.

State and Federal Policy Examples Supporting Holistic Approaches

Numerous states and the federal government have begun to enact policies that align with various components of holistic school safety, signaling a growing recognition of the need for more comprehensive strategies. These policies often address mental health services, school climate, preventative measures, and alternatives to exclusionary discipline.

Many states are mandating or funding increased access to school-based mental health professionals and the integration of Social-Emotional Learning (SEL).

Virginia, for example, has policies concerning student-to-mental health professional ratios. Tennessee directed its education department to create a conflict resolution program for K-12 students, emphasizing SEL skills. New Jersey requires annual suicide prevention instruction for public school teaching staff and promotes SEL to enhance positive school climates. Arizona expanded its School Safety Program (SSP) to include funding for school counselors and social workers. New York has made significant investments in establishing and expanding school-based mental health clinics.

Some states are encouraging or requiring schools to adopt trauma-informed approaches and restorative practices. Maryland established a Student Support Specialist Network that includes trauma-informed approaches and has policies encouraging restorative approaches before suspension or expulsion in most circumstances. Kentucky requires schools to adopt trauma-informed approaches and provide related training.

Colorado's Supportive Learning Environment for K-12 Students policy updates data frameworks to better measure and support positive school climates, requiring the collection and reporting of data on indicators like chronic absenteeism, suspensions, and expulsions.

California mandates that all K-12 schools develop and maintain Comprehensive School Safety Plans (CSSPs) designed to address campus risks, prepare for emergencies, and create safe learning environments. These plans are expected to include strategies for positive school climate, mental health interventions, restorative justice, and positive behavior interventions and supports. New York's Project SAVE (Safe Schools Against Violence in Education Act) also requires comprehensive district-wide and building-level safety plans.

West Virginia established a Safe Schools Fund for safety improvements. Arizona uses Project AWARE funds to develop mental health service infrastructure. California has made substantial investments through initiatives like the Children and Youth Behavioral Health Initiative (CYBHI) and the Community Schools Initiative (CSI) to support mental health and integrated student supports.

Current federal policy and funding support is a complicated topic, with the Department of Education having been gutted by the second Trump administration. Without a strong and centralized federal agency advocating for progressive policies in health and safety, many of the initiatives here may no longer be reliable sources.

The Bipartisan Safer Communities Act (BSCA) was a piece of federal legislation that provides significant funding that states and districts can use to hire more school counselors, social workers, and psychologists, and to implement other mental health and safety programs.

Federal relief packages, such as the American Rescue Plan's (ARPA) Elementary and Secondary School Emergency Relief (ESSER) Fund, have provided substantial resources that many states and districts have allocated towards mental health supports and SEL programs. Though these funds are no longer available, the programs and staffing that they supported were important pieces in establishing healthy school climates.

The U.S. Department of Education, prior to its destruction, offered School Climate Transformation Grants to State Educational Agencies (SEAs) and Local Educational Agencies (LEAs) to develop, enhance, or expand systems of support for implementing evidence-based, multi-tiered behavioral frameworks for improving behavioral outcomes and learning conditions.

SAMHSA established the Project AWARE (Advancing Wellness and Resilience in Education) grant program to support states and districts in increasing awareness of mental health issues among school-aged youth, providing training for school personnel, and connecting youth to services.

Bills like the Preparing Leaders to Assess Needs (PLAN) for School Safety Act aim to strengthen state-based expert centers to provide schools with greater access to resources and expertise for effective safety planning. Unfortunately, unless the federal government returns to education support and oversight, it is impossible to determine what support may be available above the state level soon.

Even without federal support, these examples illustrate a trend towards policies that recognize the multifaceted nature of school safety. However, the effectiveness of such policies often hinges not just on their mandates but on the adequacy of funding, the quality of technical assistance provided, and the flexibility allowed for local adaptation. The most promising policies act as enablers, empowering schools with the resources and guidance needed for sustainable, systemic change rather than simply imposing unfunded or overly rigid requirements.

Recommendations for Lawmakers

Lawmakers at both state and federal levels have a profound opportunity to foster a nationwide shift towards holistic school safety. By enacting supportive legislation and allocating resources strategically, they can create an environment where schools are equipped to implement comprehensive, evidence-based practices.

It is imperative that legislators at every level demand increased and sustained funding for school-based mental health services. They can work toward allocation of dedicated, sustainable funding to increase the number of school counselors, psychologists, social workers, and other mental health professionals to meet nationally recommended ratios. They can work to expand grant programs (like Project AWARE and BSCA funding) that support the development and expansion of comprehensive school mental health systems, including prevention, early intervention, and treatment services. They can demand adequate Medicaid reimbursement rates for school-based mental health services and explore options to expand eligibility for these services to all students in need, not just those with IEPs.

Particularly at the state and local level, school boards can promote and fund social-emotional learning (SEL) and positive school climate initiatives. School budgets should include funding and technical assistance for the adoption and implementation of evidence-based SEL curricula and programs as a universal, Tier 1 support.

Leaders at all levels can support state and local efforts to integrate SEL into academic instruction and schoolwide practices, and demand funding for initiatives that help schools measure and improve school climate, including the use of climate surveys and data-driven decision-making.

Supporting the implementation of trauma-informed practices and restorative justice should also be prioritized, provide resources for training all school staff in trauma-informed care and restorative practices. If possible, fund pilot programs and research to build the evidence base for restorative justice in diverse school settings.

Stakeholders at all levels should become involved in the process of reviewing and revising state and district disciplinary policies to move away from zero-tolerance approaches and encourage the use of restorative, non-exclusionary alternatives.

Further support for the holistic safety of a community includes investing in comprehensive professional development and support for educators. High-quality professional development for all school staff on holistic safety topics, including mental health awareness, SEL, trauma-informed care, restorative practices, cultural competence, and de-escalation techniques should be provided by school districts. If staff are required to locate and fund their own continuing education in addition to their already intense responsibilities, training will remain uneven and sporadic. We must support initiatives that enhance teacher and administrator training programs to include these competencies.

As communities we can foster integrated student support systems and community partnerships. If we can incentivize and fund the development of community school models and other integrated student support systems that coordinate services from education, health, and social service sectors, we can support the development of sustainable safety.

By focusing on these concepts, lawmakers can help dismantle punitive systems and build the infrastructure necessary for schools to become places where every child is not only physically safe but also emotionally supported, socially competent, and fully prepared to learn and succeed. This requires a shift from viewing safety as a standalone issue to understanding it as an integral part of a high-quality, equitable education system.

Chapter 9: Foundations of a Safe and Supportive School

In contrast to claims made by the NRA, data shows us that a truly safe school is built upon more than just physical barriers and emergency protocols. It rests on a foundation of positive relationships, a nurturing environment, and a shared sense of community. Here, we will explore two critical foundational elements: the cultivation of a positive school climate and the indispensable role of all school staff in nurturing everyday safety and well-being. These elements are not merely desirable attributes but are essential prerequisites for any effective school safety strategy.

The concept of *school climate* refers to the overall quality and character of school life, reflecting the norms, goals, values, interpersonal relationships, teaching practices, and organizational structures that define a school's environment. It is a multifaceted construct that significantly influences how students and staff experience the school day, impacting their sense of safety, belonging, and engagement. A positive school climate is not an accidental occurrence; it is intentionally built and sustained through deliberate effort and is the very bedrock upon which genuine school safety rests.

Elements of a Positive School Climate

A positive school climate is characterized by several interconnected elements that work together to create a supportive and productive learning environment.

Physical and emotional Safety are the most fundamental aspects. Students and staff must feel protected from physical harm, bullying, harassment, and discrimination. It is unrealistic to believe that these behaviors can be eliminated entirely, but students should feel that when these incidents do occur that appropriate actions will be taken to protect victims. This extends beyond the absence of overt threats to include a sense of psychological safety, where individuals feel secure enough to express themselves, take risks in their learning, and seek help without fear of negative repercussions. Clear rules, fair disciplinary practices, and well-maintained facilities contribute to this sense of safety.

A positive climate fosters a strong sense of belonging and connection among students, staff, and the wider school community. This involves encouraging student involvement in school activities and decision-making processes, promoting positive peer relationships, and ensuring that students feel known, valued, and respected by adults in the school. When students feel connected to their school, they are more likely to be engaged in their learning and contribute positively to the school community.

Schools that invest in holistic safety must also invest in relationships. This investment includes the quality of interpersonal relationships within the school—between students, between students and staff, and among staff members themselves. Respectful, trusting, and caring relationships are vital. The environment should also provide access to necessary resources that address the holistic needs of students, including academic support, counseling, and health services.

Instructional practices that are engaging, culturally responsive, and promote critical thinking contribute significantly to a positive climate. When learning is relevant to students' lives and students feel academically supported and challenged in appropriate ways, their overall experience of school is enhanced.

A clear and consistently communicated set of positive norms, values, and behavioral expectations helps to create a predictable and orderly environment. These expectations should be developed collaboratively and applied fairly to all members of the school community, including staff. Modeling respectful behavior by all adults, from administrators to support staff, is crucial in reinforcing these norms.

Each of these elements demonstrates that school climate is not an abstract ideal, but a tangible set of conditions shaped by deliberate policies, practices, and daily interactions. It is actively constructed and requires ongoing attention and commitment from the entire school community.

The Link Between Climate, Safety, and Learning

The connection between a positive school climate, student safety, and academic success is robust and well-documented. A positive school climate is not merely a pleasant backdrop for education; it is a direct and powerful contributor to both safety and learning outcomes.

When students feel supported, valued, and engaged—hallmarks of a positive school climate—they are more likely to feel safe, both physically and emotionally. This sense of safety, in turn, reduces the likelihood of negative behaviors such as bullying, aggression, and disengagement. A climate built on trust and positive relationships encourages "upstander reporting," where students feel comfortable sharing concerns about potential threats or the well-being of their peers with trusted adults, allowing for early intervention and prevention.

Research consistently links a positive school climate to a range of beneficial outcomes. Students in schools with positive climates tend to experience improved attendance rates, higher test scores, and better graduation rates, while also reporting fewer disciplinary issues. They also report lower levels of depression, anxiety, and substance use. Essentially, when students' basic needs for safety, belonging, and support are met within the school environment, their cognitive and emotional resources are freed up, allowing them to focus more effectively on learning and academic tasks. Therefore, investing in school climate is a direct investment in both student safety and academic achievement, acting as a powerful preventative measure against a range of undesired outcomes.

Strategies for Building and Sustaining a Positive Climate

Creating and maintaining a positive school climate is an ongoing process that requires intentional strategies and the active participation of all stakeholders. Several evidence-based approaches can help schools cultivate such an environment.

First, we must get comfortable with addressing conflict constructively. Conflict is inevitable, but how it is handled can significantly impact any school's climate. Implementing restorative practices, teaching conflict resolution skills, and fostering open communication can transform conflicts into learning opportunities and strengthen relationships.

Actively ensuring that all student voices are heard, valued, and incorporated into decision-making processes fosters a sense of ownership and agency. This includes creating platforms for diverse student representation and feedback mechanisms. Project-based and service learning can also boost inclusion by providing collaborative, real-world engagement opportunities.

Encouraging peer-to-peer support through mentoring programs, collaborative learning activities, and student-led initiatives can strengthen relationships and build a sense of community. Positive relationships between students and staff are equally crucial and can be nurtured through intentional interaction and empathy.

Integrating efforts to improve school climate within broader frameworks like Multi-Tiered Systems of Support (MTSS) and Positive Behavioral Interventions and Supports (PBIS) can provide a structured approach to promoting positive behaviors and addressing student needs comprehensively. Social-Emotional Learning (SEL) programs are also frequently integrated into climate improvement efforts, as they equip students with essential interpersonal and self-regulation skills.

Clear, consistent, and respectful communication among all members of the school community—students, staff, families—is foundational to building trust and collaboration. This includes sharing information about school policies, safety procedures, and climate initiatives.

School principals and leadership teams play a vital role in championing a positive school climate by building consensus around a shared vision, modeling desired behaviors, and fostering partnerships with families and the community.

These strategies are often interconnected. For instance, restorative practices inherently promote student voice and constructive conflict resolution, while SEL programs build the skills necessary for positive relationships and peer support. By adopting a comprehensive and integrated approach, schools can create a synergistic effect, where various initiatives mutually reinforce a positive and safe school climate for everyone.

Chapter 10: The Role of School Staff in Everyday Safety

While formal safety plans and designated security personnel have their place, the true fabric of a safe school is woven daily through the interactions and vigilance of every adult on campus. From the principal's office to the classroom, the cafeteria to the school bus, all school staff members play a critical role in fostering an environment where students feel secure, respected, and supported. This chapter explores how teachers, administrators, counselors, and all support staff contribute to everyday safety, emphasizing the power of relationships, the importance of empowering every adult, and the necessity of supporting staff well-being.

Teachers as Safety Architects: Building Relationships and Trust

Teachers are at the forefront of creating safe and supportive learning environments. Their daily interactions with students provide countless opportunities to build trust and positive relationships that are fundamental to psychological and emotional safety. When students trust their teachers and feel a sense of connection, they are more likely to share concerns, seek help when needed, and engage positively in the learning process.

Several practices enable teachers to become "safety architects" in their classrooms. Teachers who actively cultivate an atmosphere of respect, inclusion, and empathy create classrooms where students feel valued for who they are, are building the framework for a positive culture. This involves challenging stereotypes, addressing biases, and ensuring that all students have equitable opportunities to participate and succeed.

Simple acts like greeting students warmly, remembering their names, and showing genuine interest in their lives can significantly impact a student's sense of belonging and safety. Taking the time to understand students' individual backgrounds, strengths, and challenges allows teachers to personalize support and respond more effectively to their needs.

Teachers who communicate clearly and listen attentively to students' concerns help build trust and open lines of communication. This includes being approachable and creating opportunities for students to share their thoughts and feelings without judgment.

Teachers serve as powerful role models. By demonstrating empathy, responsible decision-making, and effective conflict resolution, they teach students valuable social and emotional skills implicitly.

Training teachers to recognize the signs of abuse, trauma, or mental health challenges, and equipping them with protocols for reporting concerns and connecting students with support services, is crucial. Strong teacher-student relationships often mean that teachers are the first to notice when a student is struggling and are often the first line of support for students without options at home.

These relationship-building efforts are not just "soft skills," they are fundamental mechanisms through which safety is established and maintained. A classroom built on trust is a classroom where students are more likely to report bullying, express anxieties, and feel safe enough to focus on learning.

Empowering All Staff: From Greetings to Guidance

School safety is a collective responsibility that extends beyond the classroom teacher to every adult member of the school community. Administrators, counselors, librarians, cafeteria workers, custodians, bus drivers, and office staff all contribute to the overall climate and safety of the school. A holistic approach to safety recognizes and empowers each of these individuals.

Ohio's comprehensive school safety framework, for example, explicitly states that creating emotional and physical safety requires the dedication and commitment of "all school staff."

In Ohio, this means all staff members should understand the school's safety protocols, their specific roles during emergencies, and how to identify and report concerns. This includes training on topics like recognizing signs of distress, de-escalation techniques, and understanding the importance of a positive school climate.

Friendly acknowledgments and warm interactions from all staff members, even during routine procedures like visitor check-ins or hallway monitoring, can help students feel more comfortable and secure. Every interaction is an opportunity to reinforce a positive and safe culture.

All staff are encouraged to be aware of their surroundings and to report any suspicious behavior, safety hazards, or concerns about student well-being through established channels. This broadens the "eyes and ears" of the school beyond designated security personnel.

While all staff share a general responsibility, specialized personnel like school counselors, psychologists, and social workers play critical leadership roles in providing mental health promotion, prevention, and support services. Effective collaboration between these specialists, teachers, and administrators is key to addressing student needs comprehensively. Even School Resource Officers (SROs), when present, should be integrated into policy-making teams with a strict focus on education, safety planning, and mentoring, rather than solely on enforcement.

This systemic view means that the "school safety team" effectively encompasses every adult in the building. When all staff members are engaged and empowered, the school's capacity to prevent incidents and respond effectively is significantly enhanced.

Supporting Teacher Well-being for a Safer School

The demands placed on educators are immense, and their own well-being is inextricably linked to their ability to create safe and supportive learning environments for students. Teachers who are stressed, burnt out, or feel unsafe themselves cannot effectively implement the very strategies that holistic safety requires. Therefore, supporting the mental health and job satisfaction of school staff is a critical, though often overlooked, component of any comprehensive school safety plan.

Strategies to support teacher well-being include nurturing strong professional relationships among teachers and between teachers and administrators creates a network of mutual support. Collaborative planning time and professional learning communities can reduce isolation and share burdens.

Just as schools provide mental wellness programs for students, similar resources should be available for staff. This can include access to counseling services, stress management workshops, and support for managing vicarious trauma.

Overwhelming workloads contribute significantly to teacher stress and burnout. School leaders should regularly assess and adjust workloads to ensure they are manageable and allow for work-life balance. Streamlining administrative tasks, as aimed for in Duneland School Corporation's MTSS implementation, can also help save teachers time and reduce stress.

Equipping teachers with the skills and knowledge to manage classroom behavior effectively, implementing SEL and restorative practices, and support students with diverse needs can increase their sense of competence and reduce stress. This includes training on culturally responsive practices and trauma-informed care.

Also important is the act of creating channels for teachers to articulate their needs, concerns, and ideas without fear of reprisal demonstrates care for their well-being and allows administrators to provide targeted support. Acknowledging the hard work and dedication of teachers through formal and informal means, and in a public way, can significantly boost morale and job satisfaction.

Investing in teacher well-being is not a peripheral concern but a direct investment in the quality of education and the safety of the school environment. Empowered, supported, and healthy educators are better equipped to build positive relationships and implement proactive strategies that lie at the heart of holistic school safety.

Part II:
A Holistic Shift

Chapter 11: Pillars of Holistic School Safety in Action

The prevention of school violence necessitates a foundational shift towards creating learning environments that are inherently supportive, safe, and engaging for all members of the school community. In this section, we will explore the core strategies that lay this groundwork, focusing on the cultivation of positive school climates, the integration of Social and Emotional Learning (SEL), the implementation of restorative practices, and the establishment of comprehensive school mental health systems. These foundational elements are not merely ancillary programs but are integral to fostering environments where violence is less likely to occur and where students are equipped with the skills and support needed to thrive.

Moving beyond the foundational elements of a positive school climate and engaged staff, this chapter addresses the specific pillars that form the active components of a holistic school safety model. These pillars represent proactive and supportive strategies designed to nurture student well-being, address conflict constructively, build strong community ties, and empower students themselves as agents of safety. Each chapter will explore a critical pillar, outlining its principles, evidence of effectiveness, and practical implementation strategies.

A student's mental and behavioral health is intrinsically linked to their ability to learn, form healthy relationships, and navigate the complexities of school life. Comprehensive mental health support within schools is not just a response to crisis but a fundamental component of creating a safe, supportive, and thriving educational environment. These supports span a continuum from universal prevention efforts that benefit all students to targeted interventions for those facing specific challenges.

The Spectrum of School-Based Mental Health Services

Effective school-based mental health services are delivered through a Multi-Tiered System of Support (MTSS), ensuring that all students receive appropriate levels of care. MTSS consists of three tiers of scaffolded support, providing leveled interventions as needed.

Tier 1 services are geared toward universal prevention and promotion. These strategies are designed for and provided to all students and aim to promote positive mental health, build social-emotional competencies, and create a supportive school climate. This level may include educating students, staff, and families about mental health, reducing stigma, and promoting help-seeking behaviors, implementing evidence-based curricula that teach skills such as self-awareness, self-management, social awareness, relationship skills, and responsible decision-making. Tier 1 is where a positive school climate is built, creating an environment that is physically and emotionally safe, respectful, and inclusive.

Tier 2 includes Early Intervention and Targeted Supports. These services are for students identified as being "at risk" of mental health challenges or who have been showing early signs of difficulty. At this level, students may be offered Small Group Interventions, focused on skill-building for issues like anxiety, stress management, or social skills deficits. Some students may be recommended for mentoring, linking at-risk students with supportive adults or older peers. Short-term individual or group counseling provided by school-employed mental health professionals, "Brief Counseling," should also be offered for students at this level of needed support.

Tier 3 supports are a set of more intensive interventions and treatment for students experiencing significant mental health needs requiring more intensive or specialized care than can be provided in most school settings. Tier 3 students may be recommended for individual therapy, ongoing counseling provided by school psychologists, social workers, or counselors, or by community mental health partners co-located at the school. In extreme situations, crisis intervention may be necessary. This would include teams established to address acute mental health crises, including suicide risk assessments and postvention support.

Collaboration with community providers, including referrals to, and coordinating care with, external mental health agencies and specialists for students requiring services beyond the school's capacity may be necessary.

School-employed mental health professionals, including school counselors, school psychologists, and school social workers, play critical leadership roles in designing, implementing, and coordinating these services. Their expertise is vital for linking mental health, behavior, environmental factors, instruction, and learning to create safe and supportive environments. Collaboration among these professionals and with teachers, administrators, and community partners is essential for a cohesive and effective system. Access to such comprehensive services has been shown to improve physical and psychological safety, academic performance, and social-emotional competence, while reducing disciplinary referrals, dropout rates, and substance abuse.

Early Intervention and Prevention Strategies

A proactive approach to student mental health emphasizes early intervention and prevention to address potential issues before they escalate into more significant problems. This involves equipping students with the skills and knowledge to navigate emotional challenges and fostering an environment that supports well-being.

Schools can implement various programs aimed at teaching students vital coping mechanisms. These programs often focus on skills such as managing stress effectively, recognizing and regulating anxiety, and developing healthy emotional responses. For instance, Tennessee passed legislation directing its department of education to create a conflict resolution program for K-12 students, designed to develop skills in communication, social interaction, and relaxation techniques. Such initiatives contribute to a healthier school environment and can reduce behavioral risks by empowering students with constructive ways to handle difficulties.

Increasing mental health literacy among students, staff, and families is another crucial prevention strategy. This involves educating the school community about common mental health conditions, the importance of seeking help, and how to access available support. By normalizing conversations about mental health and reducing associated stigma, schools can create a culture where individuals feel more comfortable acknowledging their needs and reaching out for assistance. Comprehensive school mental health systems aim to promote overall well-being and social-emotional learning, thereby reducing the prevalence and severity of mental illness from the outset. This investment in prevention and early intervention is not only beneficial for individual students but also contributes to a safer and more positive school climate for everyone. The long-term impact of such proactive measures can be significant, potentially reducing the need for more intensive and costly interventions later.

Creating Healing-Centered Environments

A significant number of students experience trauma, which can profoundly impact their behavior, learning, and overall well-being. Trauma-informed schools recognize the widespread impact of trauma and actively work to create environments that are physically and emotionally safe, supportive, and conducive to healing, rather than re-traumatizing. This approach represents a paradigm shift from asking "What's wrong with you?" to "What happened to you, and how can we help?" when addressing challenging student behaviors.

The core principles of trauma-informed care, as outlined by SAMHSA and adapted for schools, include:

- Safety: Ensuring physical and psychological safety for all students and staff.
- Trustworthiness and Transparency: Building trust through clear communication and consistent, predictable responses.
- Peer Support: Utilizing peer relationships and mutual self-help to foster a sense of community and support.
- Collaboration and Mutuality: Sharing power and decision-making among students, staff, and families.

- Empowerment, Voice, and Choice: Providing students with opportunities to have a voice, make choices, and feel a sense of control.
- Cultural, Historical, and Gender Issues: Recognizing and addressing potential biases and tailoring approaches to be culturally sensitive and responsive.
- Implementing trauma-informed practices involves several actions, often referred to as the "4 Rs":
  - <u>Realize</u> the widespread impact of trauma and understand potential paths for recovery.
  - <u>Recognize</u> the signs and symptoms of trauma in students, families, staff, and others involved with the system.
  - <u>Respond</u> by fully integrating knowledge about trauma into policies, procedures, and practices.
  - <u>Resist</u> re-traumatization by avoiding practices and environments that could trigger or exacerbate trauma responses.

Evidence suggests that trauma-informed approaches can lead to significant improvements in student behavior, including reductions in office discipline referrals, suspensions, and aggression. For example, the Healthy Environments and Response to Trauma in Schools (HEARTS) program reported substantial decreases in disciplinary incidents and suspension rates over five years. Similarly, programs like Positive Behavioral Intervention and Supports (PBIS) and Social Emotional Learning (SEL), when implemented with trauma-informed principles, have demonstrated reductions in office referrals. While meta-analyses indicate positive impacts, the rigor of some research in this area has been noted as a limitation, underscoring the need for continued methodologically sound studies. Nevertheless, the existing evidence strongly supports the value of creating healing-centered environments that acknowledge and address the impact of trauma on the school community.

Social-Emotional Learning (SEL) as a Universal Protective Factor

Social-Emotional Learning (SEL) is the process through which individuals acquire and apply the knowledge, skills, and attitudes to develop healthy identities, manage emotions, achieve personal and collective goals, feel and show empathy for others, establish and maintain supportive relationships, and make responsible and caring decisions. SEL is not just an add-on program but a foundational component of education that serves as a universal protective factor, enhancing student well-being, improving school climate, preventing violence, and boosting academic performance.

The Collaborative for Academic, Social, and Emotional Learning (CASEL) identifies five core competencies for SEL:

- Self-Awareness: Recognizing one's emotions, values, strengths, and limitations.
- Self-Management: Managing emotions, thoughts, and behaviors effectively in different situations to achieve goals and aspirations.
- Social Awareness: Understanding the perspectives of and empathizing with others, including those from diverse backgrounds and cultures.

- Relationship Skills: Establishing and maintaining healthy and supportive relationships and navigating social settings effectively.
- Responsible Decision-Making: Making caring and constructive choices about personal behavior and social interactions across diverse situations.

Evidence strongly supports the benefits of SEL. Students participating in SEL programs demonstrate improved social-emotional skills, better attitudes about themselves and others, increased prosocial behavior, and stronger connections to school. These improvements, in turn, lead to reduced behavior problems, lower emotional distress, and better academic outcomes, with some studies showing an average 11-percentile-point gain in academic achievement. Furthermore, SEL is linked to students feeling safer in school and can mitigate violence by teaching skills like self-regulation, social regulation, and problem-solving. Research also indicates a significant return on investment, with one study suggesting an $11 return for every $1 invested in SEL programming.

Chapter 12: Repairing Harm and Building Community

Traditional disciplinary systems in schools have often relied heavily on punitive measures, such as suspensions and expulsions, under the umbrella of "zero-tolerance" policies. While intended to ensure safety and order, these approaches are increasingly criticized for their ineffectiveness, their disproportionate impact on marginalized students, and their failure to address the underlying causes of misbehavior. Restorative practices offer a fundamentally different paradigm, shifting the focus from punishment to repairing harm, building relationships, and fostering a sense of community accountability.

Why Punitive Discipline Fails

Zero-tolerance policies, which mandate predetermined, often severe, consequences for specific student infractions, emerged with the aim of creating safer schools through strict rule enforcement as behavior deterrence. However, a wealth of research and experience suggests that these policies often fall short of their goals and can, in fact, be detrimental. Critics argue that zero tolerance approach does more harm than good, largely because it undermines the potential for honest interactions and relationships within the school community.

The shortcomings of punitive discipline, particularly exclusionary practices like suspension and expulsion, are numerous.

Removing students from the learning environment through suspension nearly always fails to address, even ignores, the root causes of their misbehavior and may even exacerbate problems. Students forbidden from attending school miss out on instruction, fall behind academically, and may become more disengaged from school, increasing the likelihood of repeat offenses.

Zero-tolerance policies have been consistently shown to disproportionately affect students of color, students with disabilities, and those from low-income backgrounds. This systemic inequity can lead to these students being unfairly targeted and pushed out of school, regardless of the severity or context of their actions.

The increased use of suspensions, expulsions, and school-based arrests under zero-tolerance regimes is a significant contributor to the "school-to-prison pipeline." Early and repeated exposure to exclusionary discipline and the juvenile justice system can have long-lasting negative consequences on a student's educational trajectory and life outcomes. In fact, students who interact with the juvenile justice system are more than 80 percent more likely than their peers to become involved with the justice system as adults.

An overemphasis on punishment can create a school climate characterized by fear, mistrust, and adversarial relationships between students and staff, rather than one of support and mutual respect – a polar contrast to the goals of holistic school safety.

Punitive measures typically focus on consequences rather than teaching students the social-emotional skills, conflict resolution strategies, or self-regulation techniques they may lack. Corporal punishment, for instance, has been shown to be ineffective in correcting behavior and fails to engage students in problem-solving.

The existing body of evidence strongly suggests that a purely punitive approach to discipline does not make schools safer and can actively harm students and the school community. This understanding has fueled the search for alternatives like restorative practices.

Principles and Practices of Restorative Justice in Schools

Restorative Justice (RJ), or restorative practices (RP) in the school context, offers an alternative philosophy and set of practices focused on repairing harm and strengthening relationships rather than simply assigning blame and imposing punishment.

The core principles guiding restorative approaches typically include understanding the harm caused by wrongdoing and its impact on individuals and the community, recognizing that wrongdoing creates obligations, and involving all those affected in addressing the harm and deciding on a path forward.

In schools, RP encompasses a range of proactive and reactive strategies. Community-building exercises aim to build strong relationships, foster a sense of belonging, and create a positive school climate where conflict is less likely to escalate. A significant portion of RP efforts, often cited as around 80 percent, should be proactive.

Common proactive practices include:
- Community-Building Circles: Regular opportunities for students and staff to share experiences, build trust, and establish shared values and norms.
- Affective Statements and Questions: Using "I" statements to express feelings and asking questions that encourage reflection on behavior and its impact (e.g., "What happened?" "Who has been affected?").

- Restorative Language: Integrating restorative principles into everyday communication.
- Reactive Practices (Responding to Harm): These are used when harm has occurred to address the wrongdoing, meet the needs of those harmed, and reintegrate individuals into the community. Examples include:
- Restorative Conversations/Mediation: Informal, facilitated discussions between individuals involved in conflict to understand perspectives and find solutions.
- Responsive Circles (Harm Circles): Bringing together those directly affected by an incident to discuss what happened, the impact of the harm, and what needs to be done to repair it.
- Formal Restorative Conferences: More structured meetings, often involving family members and support people, for more serious incidents, facilitated by trained individuals.

By holding students accountable in a caring and supportive way, RP aims to maintain and enhance good relationships, improve school safety, reduce exclusionary discipline, decrease misbehavior, and foster a more positive school climate. RP also complements other positive approaches like SEL and PBIS, with SEL skills being crucial for effective participation in restorative processes.

Implementing Restorative Practices

The shift from punitive to restorative approaches is a significant undertaking that requires careful planning, sustained effort, and a commitment to cultural change within the school. While the promise of RP is substantial, successful implementation faces several challenges.

All staff, not just specialists, need to understand and embrace restorative principles. Comprehensive and ongoing training is essential for developing the skills to facilitate restorative processes effectively.

RP is not a quick fix and treating its implementation as such can be harmful. Achieving desired outcomes, such as reductions in suspensions and the discipline gap, often requires long-term implementation (3+ years) with fidelity to the core principles.

School handbooks, discipline matrices, and district policies must be reviewed and revised to support and prioritize restorative responses over automatic punitive ones. This often requires community support and a Board of Education receptive of these principles.

Effective RP implementation requires dedicated personnel (e.g., restorative practice coordinators or facilitators), time for circles and conferences, and ongoing professional development, all of which have resource implications, including budgetary obligations.

Traditional disciplinary metrics (like suspension rates) may not fully capture the impact of RP, especially in the short term. Evaluations should also consider changes in school climate, relationship quality, and student/staff perceptions of safety and belonging.

Despite these challenges, numerous schools and districts have embarked on RP implementation, with varying degrees of documented success.

In the Oakland Unified School District (OUSD), California, they have established a long-standing commitment to restorative justice. Their implementation guide emphasizes building relationships, respectful dialogue, participatory decision-making, and addressing underlying causes of conflict.

An evaluation of their school Violence Intervention and Prevention (VIP) program, which incorporates restorative events, showed early positive indicators like high life-goal completion for participating students and increased student knowledge of how to access help, though significant impacts on broader academic or disciplinary outcomes were not yet evident in limited early data.

In Texas, the Austin Independent School District's (AISD), Education Innovation and Research (EIR) grant funded a Culturally Responsive Restorative Practices (CRRP) program in 10 schools.

An evaluation by the American Institutes for Research (AIR) found that while CRRP gained traction, it was not yet fully ingrained, partly due to the COVID-19 pandemic. Quantitatively, the evaluation did not show strong overall effects on discipline or achievement but did find that students in CRRP schools perceived relationships with adults more favorably and that certain student subgroups (e.g., Native American, Asian, multiracial students) had fewer disciplinary incidents. Qualitative data from students and teachers was more positive, highlighting improved relationships and classroom climate.

In Minnesota, Minneapolis Public Schools (MPS), partnered with the Legal Rights Center to offer a Family and Youth Restorative Conference Program for students facing expulsion recommendations.

A pilot evaluation of this program (2010-2012) showed high levels of satisfaction among students and parents, positive increases in family communication, and for students who remained in MPS, improved attendance and decreased involvement in serious behavioral incidents (suspensions) in the year following participation.

New York City Schools underwent evaluation of an RJ program in several NYC schools that found widespread perceptions of an improved school climate among participants. However, it reported little impact on the reliance on suspensions, leading researchers to suggest that metrics more aligned with RJ's broader goals (like relationship quality and climate) should be considered alongside traditional disciplinary data.

In the West Linn-Wilsonville School District of Oregon they outline a restorative approach that includes collaborative meetings, linking consequences to repairing harm and learning new skills, actively including student voices in developing consequences, and structured processes for welcoming students back and restoring relationships after an incident.

These examples underscore that the success of RP is highly context-dependent and relies on sustained commitment, adequate resources, and a willingness to adapt practices to the specific needs of the school community. It is a journey toward a more relational and supportive school culture, not simply the adoption of a new set of disciplinary tools. The focus must be on building community and addressing the underlying causes of conflict, with the understanding that this proactive work is the foundation for effectively repairing harm when it occurs.

These practices, when implemented thoughtfully and consistently, can transform a school's approach to discipline, moving from a cycle of punishment to one of learning, repair, and community strengthening.

Chapter 13: Strong Partnerships, Safe Schools

Schools do not exist in isolation. They are integral parts of wider communities, and their success in creating safe and supportive environments is significantly enhanced when they forge strong partnerships with families and local organizations. Engaging parents as essential allies and leveraging the diverse resources available within the community are critical components of a holistic approach to school safety. These collaborations can extend the school's capacity to support student well-being, provide a broader network of care, and ensure that safety initiatives are responsive to the needs and values of the entire community.

Engaging Parents as Essential Partners in School Safety

Parents and caregivers are their children's first and most enduring educators and advocates. Their involvement in school safety efforts is not just beneficial but essential for creating environments where students feel truly secure and supported. Meaningful parent engagement moves beyond traditional, often passive, roles like attending parent-teacher conferences or volunteering for bake sales, to encompass authentic partnership in decision-making, policy development, and the co-creation of a safe school culture.

Schools must work to establish consistent and accessible channels for two-way communication with families regarding safety and well-being. This includes proactively sharing information about safety policies, emergency procedures, and climate initiatives, as well as actively soliciting feedback and concerns from parents. Using multiple communication methods (email, newsletters, phone calls, parent portals, social media, etc.) and providing information in multiple languages can ensure broader reach. It is vital that the community be understood as a multicultural body, and that there be awareness of, and materials designed for, the languages spoken in the homes of students throughout the district.

Parents, and students, are more likely to engage when they feel welcomed, respected, and valued by the school. This involves creating a positive school climate for families, offering diverse opportunities for involvement, and ensuring equitable access for all parents, regardless of background, language, or socioeconomic status. Providing translation services, flexible meeting times, and even childcare or transportation for school events can remove significant barriers to participation.

Parents should be included on school safety committees and involved in the development and review of safety plans and policies. Their input should also be sought by local Boards of Education, through surveys, focus groups, or other solicitation of feedback. Their perspectives on community conditions, student needs, and potential solutions are important, but should not be held above expert recommendations. Rather, feedback should be used to identify deficiencies in public understanding of best practices and shape the ways in which information is delivered to the community. The National PTA provides a blueprint for parents to engage with legislators on these issues, emphasizing the power of personal stories and specific asks related to mental health, restorative justice, and balanced security measures.

Schools can also empower parents by providing them with information and resources on topics such as how to talk to their children about safety, recognizing warning signs of distress or risk, understanding cyber safety, and supporting their child's social-emotional development. Hosting informational sessions, workshops, or "safety fairs" can be effective ways to disseminate this information.

Schools can encourage parents to become active participants in safety initiatives, such as volunteering for safety-related tasks (if permissible in the district), and to advocate for holistic safety approaches within the school and to policymakers. Programs like "Parents for Safer Schools" aim to equip parents with the knowledge and tools to become more effective advocates for their own children and their communities.

When parents are actively and meaningfully engaged, they become crucial allies in reinforcing safety messages at home, identifying emerging concerns early, supporting school initiatives, and contributing to a stronger, more cohesive school community. Research indicates that such involvement is linked not only to improved safety but also to better academic outcomes and social-emotional skills for students.

Leveraging Community Resources and Programs

No school can single-handedly meet all the complex needs of its students and families. Holistic school safety requires the willingness to look beyond the school walls to leverage the wealth of resources and expertise available within the broader community. Partnerships with local community organizations, health and mental health providers, businesses, and other entities can significantly expand a school's capacity to provide comprehensive support.

To this end, schools might proactively identify local organizations and services that can support student well-being, such as mental health clinics, youth development programs, family support services, libraries, senior-serving organizations, and others. Other community elements should also be considered, including options for youth entertainment and recreation; a community that offers no healthy recreative outlets for its youth is ensuring that young people will find their own, less healthy, outlets for their energies.

Collaboration with community partners should be intentional and goal oriented. Schools should select partners whose missions align with the school's safety and well-being objectives and whose services meet identified student and family needs. Formalizing these partnerships through Memoranda of Understanding (MOUs) can clarify roles, responsibilities, communication protocols, and resource sharing. These MOUs also become a form a visible assurance for families that these arrangements are appropriately managed.

Another powerful example of how schools can serve as hubs to integrate academic, health, and social services through partnerships with community agencies is through the Community Schools model. California's Community Schools Partnership Program, for instance, leverages local partnerships to provide supportive services, particularly in high-need areas, improving access to support like health care, mental health services, and family engagement programs. The Chicago Public Schools' Community Schools Initiative (CSI) similarly invests in partnerships with community-based organizations to address students' academic, social, and emotional needs.

Bringing community-based services directly into the school building, such as establishing school-based health or mental health clinics run by community providers, can reduce barriers to access for students and families. The demand for behavioral healthcare professionals for youth has never been greater, and the field has never been stretched further. By bringing these partners into schools, families can avoid the barriers of time, availability, cost, and stigma by making behavioral health part of the school day.

In some instances, community members can contribute valuable time and expertise as volunteers, mentors, or guest speakers, enriching the school environment and providing additional adult support for students. Schools can partner with community groups to co-host workshops, awareness campaigns (e.g., on substance abuse prevention or mental health awareness), and events that promote safety and well-being for the entire community.

These partnerships can transform schools into vital community hubs, creating a more robust and responsive network of support that extends beyond the traditional school day and campus boundaries.

Collaborative Models for Student Well-being (including law enforcement in non-security roles)

Creating a comprehensive system of support for student well-being requires effective collaboration among various stakeholders, each bringing unique expertise and resources. This often involves multidisciplinary teams within the school and strategic partnerships with external entities, including, at times, law enforcement agencies engaged in supportive, non-punitive capacities.

The key to successful collaboration is a shared vision and clearly defined roles. Within the school, teams comprising administrators, teachers, counselors, school psychologists, social workers, and other specialized instructional support personnel work together to implement MTSS, identify student needs, and coordinate interventions.

When involving external partners, particularly law enforcement, it is crucial to redefine roles to align with a holistic safety approach. The critiques of SROs often stem from their involvement in routine school discipline, which can lead to the criminalization of student behavior and negatively impact school climate. However, several holistic models advocate for partnerships with law enforcement that are carefully circumscribed and focused on specific areas.

Law enforcement agencies, for example, possess critical expertise in crisis response. Schools should collaborate with police, fire, and emergency medical services to develop and practice comprehensive emergency operations plans. This includes conducting joint drills and establishing clear communication protocols for emergencies.

Multidisciplinary threat assessment teams often include representatives from law enforcement alongside educators and mental health professionals. These teams work to identify, assess, and manage potential threats in a non-punitive, preventive manner, focusing on providing support and intervention to at-risk individuals.

Law enforcement can be valuable partners in providing safety-related training to staff and students (on active shooter response options, if deemed appropriate by the school community and aligned with best practices that avoid undue trauma) and participating in community outreach efforts to build positive relationships. Ohio's framework, for instance, envisions SROs as members of policy-making teams focused on safety planning, education, and mentoring, rather than primarily discipline.

When SROs or other law enforcement personnel are present in schools, MOUs should clearly delineate their roles and responsibilities, emphasizing that they should not be involved in routine age-appropriate, non-criminal, school disciplinary matters that are best handled by educators. Their role must be one of support to the educational mission and the creation of a positive school climate, not undermining it.

The goal of these collaborations is to leverage the unique strengths of each partner to create a comprehensive safety net. For law enforcement, this means shifting engagement from a model of daily policing within schools to one of strategic partnership focused on prevention, preparedness, and crisis response, always in support of the school's primary mission of education and well-being. This nuanced approach allows schools to benefit from law enforcement expertise where appropriate, without compromising the supportive and trusting environment essential for holistic safety.

Chapter 14: Amplifying Student Voices for Safer Schools

Students are not passive recipients of school safety measures; they are active stakeholders with unique perspectives and invaluable insights into the dynamics of their school environment. A truly holistic approach to school safety recognizes the critical importance of student voice and actively seeks to involve students in planning, decision-making, and leadership roles. When students are empowered to contribute to their own safety and the well-being of their peers, the effectiveness of safety initiatives is enhanced, and a stronger, more inclusive school culture is fostered.

The Importance of Student Involvement in Safety Planning

Engaging students in safety planning is more than a symbolic gesture; it is a strategic imperative for creating genuinely safe and responsive school environments. Students often possess a nuanced understanding of peer dynamics, potential risks, and the day-to-day realities of school life that adults may not fully perceive. Their direct experiences can illuminate vulnerabilities and highlight areas where safety measures may be falling short or having unintended negative consequences.

The benefits of meaningful student involvement are numerous. When students contribute to the design of safety plans and initiatives, the resulting measures are more likely to be relevant, practical, and accepted by the student body. Their understanding of peer culture can lead to more effective communication strategies and interventions.

Student participation in these processes fosters a sense of ownership and shared responsibility for school safety among students. When they have a voice in creating the rules and norms, they are more invested in upholding them.

Involving students in decision-making contributes to a stronger sense of belonging, agency, and empowerment, which are key components of a positive school climate. When students feel heard and respected, trust between students and staff is strengthened. Students are often the first to know about potential threats, bullying, or peers who are struggling. Creating safe and trusted channels for students to report concerns, and involving them in promoting such reporting, can be crucial for early intervention.

These are also important in the development of our future community leaders. Participating in safety planning and related activities helps students develop valuable leadership, communication, problem-solving, and advocacy skills.

Ignoring student perspectives or treating them as passive subjects of adult-devised plans, is a missed opportunity. Holistic safety requires moving beyond simply informing students about safety rules to actively co-creating safe and supportive school communities *with* them.

Models for Meaningful Student Participation and Leadership

Schools can implement various structures and initiatives to ensure that student voices are meaningfully incorporated into safety efforts and that students have opportunities to develop leadership skills in this domain. These are not limited to the realm of school safety, they can be important tools for every aspect of a positive school climate.

Forming dedicated committees where students work alongside staff, administrators, and sometimes parents to discuss safety concerns, review policies, and propose solutions is a direct way to involve them in governance. These committees should have diverse representation of the student body to capture a wide range of student experiences. Washoe County School District, for example, holds a "Strength in Voices Symposium" where students analyze climate survey data and make recommendations, and students also serve on staff committees.

Empowering student government associations to take an active role in promoting school safety and a positive climate, and creating other leadership opportunities focused on these areas, can amplify student influence.

Peer-led programs are also an invaluable resource for safety, substance use prevention, and other positive behavior foundations. Training students to mediate conflicts among their peers can provide a less formal and often more effective way to resolve disputes before they escalate.

Older students can mentor younger students, providing guidance, support, and positive role modeling, which can enhance feelings of connectedness and safety.

Students can lead campaigns to raise awareness about issues like bullying prevention, mental health, or online safety, using language and approaches that resonate with their peers. The Safe and Sound Student Club Program Kit is one resource that supports such initiatives.

Regular school climate surveys are vital tools in creating sustainable cultures. Surveying students about their perceptions of safety, belonging, and school climate, and then using this data (with student involvement in its analysis and interpretation) to inform improvement efforts, is crucial.

In schools implementing restorative justice, students' voices are central to processes like circles and conferences, where they share their experiences, discuss harm, and participate in developing solutions.

Supporting student-initiated clubs or projects focused on promoting kindness, inclusion, mental wellness, or specific safety concerns can foster student agency and leadership.

These models demonstrate that providing structured opportunities for student participation not only improves the immediate school environment but also serves as a valuable educational experience. By engaging in these roles, students learn to analyze problems, collaborate with diverse groups, advocate for change, and take responsibility for their communities—skills that are essential for active citizenship and future leadership.

Chapter 15: Cultivating Positive School Climates

A positive school climate is the bedrock upon which effective violence prevention efforts are built. It encompasses the quality and character of school life, reflecting the extent to which students and staff feel physically and emotionally safe, supported, respected, and engaged in the learning environment. We will examine the principles of such an environment, examine the crucial roles of school leadership and staff buy-in, and explore the importance of student voice and engagement in shaping a positive climate.

Principles of a Safe and Supportive Learning Environment

A safe and supportive learning environment is characterized by several key principles that work in concert to promote student well-being and academic success. Fundamentally, it is an environment where students feel both physically and emotionally secure. Physical safety involves protection from harm and secure facilities, while emotional safety pertains to an atmosphere free from intimidation, harassment, and fear, where students feel comfortable expressing themselves and taking academic risks.

Engagement is another critical principle. This involves actively encouraging student involvement in school activities, decision-making processes, and their own learning. When students are engaged, they develop a stronger sense of belonging and connection to the school community, which is a protective factor against violence and disaffection.

Support is the third cornerstone. This includes not only academic support to help students achieve their potential but also includes social and emotional support to help them navigate challenges and develop healthy coping mechanisms. Supportive relationships—between students and teachers, among students, and between the school and families—are vital. The environment must also provide access to resources that address the holistic needs of students, encompassing their academic, social, emotional, behavioral, and mental health.

Research consistently links a positive school climate to a host of beneficial outcomes, including higher attendance rates, improved test scores, increased promotion and graduation rates, and reduced levels of violence and bullying. Therefore, cultivating such a climate is not merely an ideal but a practical necessity for effective schools. It acts as an active agent in violence prevention, as students who feel safe, supported, and connected are less likely to engage in aggressive behavior and more likely to report concerns, contributing to a self-reinforcing cycle of safety and positivity. The interdependence of these principles (safety, support, and engagement) means that efforts to improve school climate must be comprehensive, addressing all dimensions simultaneously to achieve the greatest impact.

The Role of School Leadership and Staff Buy-in

The cultivation of a positive school climate and the successful implementation of violence prevention strategies are heavily reliant on the active involvement and commitment of school leadership and the entire school staff. School leaders, including principals and administrators, play a pivotal role in championing these initiatives, setting a clear vision, and allocating the necessary resources. Their visible support and advocacy are essential for fostering a school-wide culture that prioritizes safety, respect, and emotional well-being. Effective leadership in this context extends beyond administrative duties to active culture-building, where leaders consistently communicate the importance of a positive school climate and model the desired behaviors and attitudes. Without this strong, proactive leadership, even well-designed programs can falter due to a lack of coherent direction or sustained institutional support.

Equally crucial is securing buy-in and active participation from all school staff, including teachers, counselors, support staff, and non-teaching personnel. When staff members understand the rationale behind school climate initiatives, feel invested in their success, and are equipped with the necessary training and skills, they become powerful agents of positive change. Conversely, a lack of staff buy-in or inconsistent implementation of agreed-upon practices can send mixed messages to students and undermine the effectiveness of any program. Therefore, efforts to improve school climate must include robust professional development that not only imparts skills but also builds understanding, commitment, and a sense of shared ownership among staff. Addressing staff concerns, providing ongoing support, and creating collaborative platforms for problem-solving are key strategies for fostering this essential buy-in.

Student Engagement and Voice in Climate Building

Actively involving students in shaping their school environment is a powerful strategy for fostering a positive and safer school climate. Students are not merely passive recipients of the school environment; they are key stakeholders whose perspectives, experiences, and contributions are invaluable in creating a community where everyone feels respected and valued. Providing students with genuine opportunities to voice their concerns, share their ideas, and participate in decision-making processes that affect their school lives can significantly enhance their sense of belonging, ownership, and responsibility.

When students are engaged as leaders, problem-solvers, and decision-makers within their classrooms and the broader school community, as advocated by SEL-focused school models, they are more likely to be invested in the school's success and the well-being of its members. This sense of agency can translate into greater adherence to school norms, more positive peer interactions, and an increased willingness to contribute to a safe and supportive atmosphere. For example, involving students in school safety initiatives, student councils, or climate committees can play a pivotal role in raising awareness and preventing acts of violence.

For student engagement to be truly effective, it must be authentic and move beyond tokenism. This means creating structures and processes that genuinely empower students to influence decisions, providing them with the necessary skills and support to participate meaningfully, and ensuring that adults in the school community listen to and seriously consider their input. Superficial attempts at student engagement can breed cynicism and disengagement, whereas authentic partnership can unlock significant positive potential, transforming students into active co-creators of a thriving school climate.

Chapter 16: Social and Emotional Learning (SEL)

Social and Emotional Learning (SEL) is increasingly recognized as a fundamental component of education and a cornerstone of effective school violence prevention. SEL is the process through which individuals acquire and apply the knowledge, skills, and attitudes to develop healthy identities, manage emotions, achieve personal and collective goals, feel and show empathy for others, establish and maintain supportive relationships, and make responsible and caring decisions. This chapter will explore the CASEL framework, examine evidence-based SEL curricula, discuss the importance of systemic SEL implementation, and address the complexities of measuring SEL outcomes while ensuring equity.

The CASEL Framework: Core Competencies

The Collaborative for Academic, Social, and Emotional Learning (CASEL) has developed a widely adopted framework that organizes SEL into five core, interrelated competence areas. This framework provides a comprehensive structure for understanding and implementing SEL initiatives. These competencies are foundational for positive youth development and are directly linked to behaviors that can prevent violence and promote a positive school environment.

The five core competencies are:
- Self-Awareness: The ability to understand one's own emotions, thoughts, and values and how they influence behavior across contexts. This includes recognizing one's strengths and limitations with a well-grounded sense of confidence and purpose.

- Self-Management: The ability to manage one's emotions, thoughts, and behaviors effectively in different situations and to achieve goals and aspirations. This includes the capacity to delay gratification, manage stress, and feel motivation and agency.
- Social Awareness: The ability to understand the perspectives of and empathize with others, including those from diverse backgrounds, cultures, and contexts. This includes the capacity to feel compassion for others and understand broader historical and social norms for behavior.
- Relationship Skills: The ability to establish and maintain healthy and supportive relationships and to effectively navigate settings with diverse individuals and groups. This includes communicating clearly, listening actively, cooperating, and negotiating conflict constructively.
- Responsible Decision-Making: The ability to make caring and constructive choices about personal behavior and social interactions across diverse situations. This includes considering ethical standards, safety concerns, and the consequences of actions for oneself, others, and the community.

These competencies are not developed in isolation but are interconnected, mutually reinforcing skills that contribute to overall social-emotional well-being. For instance, effective self-management of emotions relies on accurate self-awareness, and strong relationship skills are built upon social awareness and empathy. By systematically teaching these skills, SEL programs act as a primary prevention strategy, equipping students with the internal tools to navigate social challenges constructively, manage their impulses, and make choices that reduce the likelihood of aggressive or violent behavior. CASEL also emphasizes that SEL advances educational equity and excellence through authentic school-family-community partnerships that establish supportive learning environments.

Evidence-Based SEL Curricula

Numerous evidence-based SEL curricula have been developed to explicitly teach these core competencies. Two prominent examples often cited are Promoting Alternative THinking Strategies (PATHS) and the RULER approach.

PATHS (Promoting Alternative THinking Strategies) is a curriculum designed for elementary school children that focuses on developing self-control, emotional literacy, social competence, positive peer relations, and interpersonal problem-solving skills. Program developers for PATHS report a range of positive outcomes, including significant improvements in students' ability to tolerate frustration, use effective conflict-resolution strategies, and a 32 percent reduction in teacher-reported aggressive behavior. They also cite gains in academic engagement and achievement test scores.

However, it is important to note the complexities in evaluating SEL programs. For instance, a review by the What Works Clearinghouse (WWC), which applies rigorous standards for research, found that the studies on PATHS meeting their criteria showed "no discernible effects" on academic achievement, social interactions, observed individual behavior, or emotional status for the grade levels examined. This discrepancy highlights the challenge of measuring SEL impact consistently and the importance of considering the source and methodology of effectiveness studies. Factors such as fidelity of implementation, teacher training, and the specific school context can significantly influence program outcomes.

RULER (Recognizing, Understanding, Labeling, Expressing, and Regulating emotions), developed at the Yale Center for Emotional Intelligence, is another widely implemented SEL approach. RULER emphasizes the development of emotional intelligence through its five core skills. Research on RULER suggests positive impacts on school climate, including enhanced emotional support and better classroom organization. Students in RULER classrooms have shown improved academic performance, particularly in English Language Arts, and teachers have rated them as having better work habits and conduct. Studies also indicate that RULER can lead to less bullying and aggressive behavior. A key component of RULER is the development of a nuanced emotional vocabulary ("Feeling Words"), as the ability to accurately label emotions is considered crucial for understanding and managing them effectively. This focus on precise emotional language can empower students with greater self-awareness and more effective self-regulation strategies.

The varying findings on programs like PATHS underscore the need for careful selection and implementation of SEL curricula, continuous monitoring, and adaptation to specific school contexts to maximize their potential benefits.

Systemic SEL Implementation

For Social and Emotional Learning to achieve its full potential in fostering positive student development and preventing violence, it must be implemented systemically, becoming an integral part of the entire school culture, rather than being confined to isolated lessons or programs. A whole-school approach to SEL ensures that principles of social and emotional competence are woven into all aspects of students' educational experiences, across classrooms, school-wide policies and practices, and in partnership with families and communities.

Systemic SEL relies on district and state leaders to align policies, resources, and actions to support a coordinated learning process. This involves several key elements:

A critical, yet often overlooked, aspect of systemic SEL is the development of social and emotional competencies in adults within the school system. Educators and staff who are themselves socially and emotionally competent, and whose well-being is supported, are better equipped to model SEL skills, build trusting relationships with students, and create supportive learning environments. Investing in adult SEL is thus a prerequisite for effective student SEL.

SEL programs and practices must be both evidence-based and culturally responsive, acknowledging and valuing the diverse backgrounds and experiences of students. A one-size-fits-all approach is unlikely to be effective; SEL initiatives should be adapted to be meaningful within the local context and to promote equitable outcomes for all students.

SEL should not be seen as separate from academics, instead, these skills should be explicitly taught and integrated into instruction across all subject areas. Furthermore, SEL principles should inform school-wide practices, including discipline policies, student support systems, and interactions in common areas like hallways and cafeterias.

Systemic SEL involves the ongoing collection and analysis of data to monitor implementation quality, assess student outcomes, and identify areas for improvement. This data-driven approach allows schools and districts to refine their SEL strategies and ensure they are meeting the needs of their students.

A core goal of systemic SEL is to create an inclusive school culture where all students feel safe, respected, supported, and have a sense of belonging. This includes prioritizing student agency and providing opportunities for students to have a voice in their learning and school environment.

Recognizing that learning and development occur across multiple settings, systemic SEL emphasizes strong, collaborative partnerships between schools, families, and community organizations. Aligning efforts and communication across these settings reinforces SEL skills and provides a more holistic support system for students.

CASEL's framework for systemic SEL, developed through years of research and collaboration with school districts, provides a roadmap for these efforts, focusing on building a strong foundation, strengthening adult SEL, promoting SEL for students, and practicing continuous improvement. By adopting such a comprehensive and integrated approach, SEL can become a powerful lever for positive change in schools, contributing to improved academic outcomes, enhanced student well-being, and safer learning environments.

Measuring SEL Outcomes and Ensuring Equity

Assessing Social and Emotional Learning (SEL) competencies and the effectiveness of SEL programs presents unique complexities. Unlike academic subjects with standardized tests, SEL involves multifaceted skills and attitudes that can be challenging to quantify. Moreover, ensuring that SEL assessment practices are equitable, culturally responsive, and genuinely beneficial to students is paramount.

Effective SEL assessment begins with a clear vision and intentionality, with assessment goals directly tied to the broader organizational vision for SEL. Practitioners emphasize that SEL assessment should be strengths-based, focusing on identifying and building upon the social and emotional assets that all individuals possess, rather than adopting a deficit-oriented approach that identifies weaknesses. This strength-based perspective is particularly crucial for equity, as it helps to avoid disproportionately labeling students from marginalized backgrounds.

Several best practices guide the design and implementation of SEL measures. Measures should align with a recognized SEL framework (like CASEL's) and any relevant K-12 SEL standards.

Equity and cultural responsiveness is a also critical consideration. Strategies to ensure equity include involving diverse stakeholders in measure development, conducting cognitive interviews with representative student groups during piloting, and using statistical techniques like differential item functioning analysis to identify potential bias.

While self-report surveys are commonly used due to their scalability and cost-effectiveness, they are susceptible to response biases (social desirability, reference bias, etc.). Innovative formats such as direct assessments, behavioral observations, situational judgment tasks, and forced-choice items are being explored to mitigate these biases, though they may present logistical challenges.

Any measures of SEL programs should be tailored to the developmental stages of students, as children and youth experience and express social and emotional competencies differently at various ages. SEL measurements themselves require ongoing refinement. Pilot testing changes and utilizing methods like Item Response Theory (IRT) for scoring can help maintain comparability over time while improving measure quality. Developing an item bank can also prevent question staleness.

A significant consideration is the use of SEL data. While SEL measures can be valuable for progress monitoring and guiding continuous improvement of programs and supports, there is a consensus among researchers that current self-report SEL surveys and their growth measures are not yet robust enough for high-stakes accountability decisions, such as school ratings or teacher evaluations. The risk of "teaching to the test" for SEL or misinterpreting data in high-stakes contexts is a serious concern. Therefore, the primary use of SEL assessment data should be formative, aimed at understanding student needs, tailoring interventions, and improving the quality of SEL implementation, always with a commitment to guarding against bias and protecting student privacy.

Chapter 17: Restorative Practices

Restorative Practices (RP), often referred to as Restorative Justice in school settings, offer a transformative approach to addressing conflict and misbehavior. Instead of focusing solely on punishment for wrongdoing, RP centers on repairing harm, rebuilding relationships, and fostering a sense of community accountability and dialogue. This chapter will explore the core principles of RP, examine various models like circles and conferences, present evidence of their impact on school discipline and climate, and discuss the challenges and best practices associated with their implementation.

Principles of Restorative Justice in Schools

Restorative Justice (RJ) in schools is fundamentally about addressing harm and promoting healing within the school community. It operates on a set of core principles that distinguish it from purely punitive approaches to discipline.

The primary goal of RJ is to address the harm caused by an incident, considering the needs of those who were harmed (victims), those who caused the harm (offenders), and the wider school community. The emphasis is on making things right to the greatest extent possible.

RJ recognizes that misconduct often damages relationships, so a key objective is to mend these broken connections and strengthen the fabric of the school community. This involves fostering empathy, understanding, and reconciliation.

Accountability in RJ means taking responsibility for one's actions and understanding their impact on others. It is not merely about accepting punishment but about actively participating in repairing the harm and committing to positive behavioral change.

RJ processes are typically dialogic, bringing together those affected by an incident to share their perspectives, express their feelings, and collaboratively determine how to address the harm. This inclusive approach aims to give voice to all parties involved.

The proactive potential of RJ must not be overlooked. While RJ can be a reactive response to conflict, it is also a proactive approach to building a strong, supportive, and respectful school community where conflicts are less likely to escalate into serious harm.

The implementation of RJ in schools represents a cultural shift, moving away from a mindset where misbehavior is seen primarily as rule-breaking requiring punishment, towards one where it is viewed as an opportunity for learning, growth, and community strengthening. This often involves seeing "bad behavior" as indicative of a missing skill that needs to be taught, rather than a deliberate choice to cause harm.

While RJ does not preclude consequences, it prioritizes understanding the root causes of behavior and ensuring that individuals learn from their mistakes and make amends. The proactive dimension of RP is crucial; by investing in relationship-building and community norms, schools can prevent many conflicts from arising or escalating.

Models of Restorative Practices (Circles, Conferences, Peer Mediation)

Schools employ a variety of models and techniques to implement restorative practices, ranging from proactive community-building activities to responsive interventions for addressing harm. These practices form a continuum, allowing schools to tailor their approach to different situations and student needs.

- Restorative Circles (Community-Building and Reentry Circles): Circles are a versatile tool used for both proactive community building and responding to conflict. In a circle format, participants (students and staff) sit facing each other, often passing a talking piece to ensure everyone has an opportunity to speak and be heard without interruption.
- Community-Building Circles: Used regularly in classrooms (e.g., daily morning meetings), these circles aim to build empathy, trust, and positive relationships among students and between students and teachers. They can be used to share feelings, discuss values, set classroom norms, and foster a sense of belonging.
- Responsive Circles (Problem-Solving or Healing Circles): When harm has occurred, circles can be used to bring together those affected to discuss the incident, its impact, and how to repair the harm. This process encourages accountability and collaborative problem-solving.
- Reentry Circles: These are used to support a student's return to the school community after an

absence due to suspension or other reasons, helping to mend relationships and ensure a smoother transition.

- Restorative Conferences: These are more formal, structured meetings typically used for more serious incidents of harm. A restorative conference brings together the person(s) who caused harm, those who were harmed, and their respective supporters (e.g., family members, friends, school staff). Led by a trained facilitator, the conference provides a safe space for all parties to share their perspectives on what happened, how they were affected, and what needs to be done to repair the harm. The process often culminates in a mutually agreed-upon plan of action for the person who caused harm to make amends.
- Peer Mediation: This model trains students to act as neutral third-party facilitators to help their peers resolve conflicts peacefully. Peer mediators guide disputants through a structured process of communication, helping them to understand each other's perspectives and collaboratively develop their own solutions. This approach not only helps resolve immediate conflicts but also empowers students by teaching them valuable communication, problem-solving, and conflict-resolution skills. It can reduce reliance on adult intervention for minor disputes and foster a greater sense of student ownership over the school climate.

- Affective Statements (or "I" Statements): A foundational communication tool in restorative practices, affective statements involve expressing one's feelings and the impact of another's behavior without blaming or judging. For example, instead of saying "You're being disruptive," a teacher might say, "When I hear talking while I'm giving instructions, I feel frustrated because I'm worried students won't understand the assignment." This models respectful communication and helps individuals understand the consequences of their actions.
- Active Listening: This involves paying close attention to what others are saying, both verbally and nonverbally, and demonstrating understanding and empathy. It is a core skill for all restorative processes.

These various models and techniques provide schools with a flexible toolkit to build a restorative culture, prevent harm, and respond to conflicts in a way that promotes learning, accountability, and stronger relationships.

Impact on School Discipline, Behavior, and Climate

A growing body of research suggests that the implementation of restorative practices can have a significant positive impact on school discipline, student behavior, and overall school climate. By shifting the focus from punishment to repairing harm and building relationships, these practices aim to create more supportive and equitable learning environments.

Studies have demonstrated that restorative practices can lead to notable improvements in student behavior and a reduction in disciplinary issues. For instance, research indicates that RP can effectively reduce anxiety, stress, and aggressive behavior among students, while concurrently decreasing school violence. Schools that adopt restorative approaches often see a decrease in fighting and bullying, as well as fewer office referrals and classroom removals. This reduction in disruptive behaviors contributes to a more orderly and focused learning environment.

One of the most significant impacts of restorative practices is the reduction in exclusionary discipline, such as suspensions and expulsions. A study in Chicago Public Schools found that the rollout of RP led to an 18 percent decline in suspension days and a 19 percent decrease in overall student arrests. This is particularly important given the disproportionate rates at which students of color and students with disabilities are subjected to exclusionary discipline. By offering alternatives to suspension, restorative practices can help disrupt the school-to-prison pipeline, keeping students engaged in their education and reducing their contact with the juvenile justice system.

Beyond disciplinary outcomes, restorative practices contribute to a more positive school climate. Students in schools with RP report improved relationships with teachers and peers, an enhanced sense of belonging, and increased feelings of safety. This improved climate, characterized by trust and mutual respect, not only makes school a more pleasant place to be but also creates conditions more conducive to learning. The interplay between an improved climate and reduced violence appears to be reciprocal: a better climate reduces conflict, and the restorative process of addressing conflicts further strengthens relationships and community trust.

Furthermore, exposure to restorative practices has been linked to improved academic outcomes, with particularly strong positive effects observed for Black and Latino/a students, suggesting that RP can play a role in reducing achievement gaps. Declines in student misbehavior, gang membership, victimization, depressive symptoms, and substance abuse have also been associated with the increased use of restorative practices in schools.

Challenges and Best Practices in Implementation

Despite the promising outcomes, the implementation of restorative justice in schools is a complex endeavor fraught with potential challenges. Successfully embedding these practices requires more than superficial adoption; it demands a systemic shift in school culture, policies, and adult mindsets.

Common challenges include:
- Treating RJ as a Quick Fix: Schools may adopt RJ with unrealistic expectations of immediate reductions in suspensions without committing to the deeper cultural changes required.
- Lack of Staff Buy-in and Understanding: If teachers and administrators do not fully understand or support the philosophy of RJ, implementation will likely be inconsistent and ineffective. Resistance can stem from a preference for punitive measures or a lack of confidence in restorative techniques.
- Inconsistent Application: If RJ practices are not applied uniformly across the school, or if they are

used selectively, students may receive mixed messages, undermining the program's credibility.
- Neglecting Underlying Causes of Misbehavior: RJ focuses on repairing harm, but if the root causes of a student's behavior (e.g., trauma, unmet needs, skill deficits) are not also addressed, the problematic behavior is likely to recur.
- Insufficient Follow-Up: Restorative processes are not one-time events. Lack of follow-up to ensure agreements are met and relationships are truly mended can diminish long-term impact.
- Resource and Training Needs: Effective RJ requires significant investment in training for all staff, ongoing coaching, and potentially dedicated personnel to facilitate more intensive restorative processes.
- Societal Resistance: A broader societal preference for retributive justice can create resistance to restorative approaches within the school community.
- Managing Power Imbalances: Ensuring that restorative processes are fair and that all voices are heard, especially when power imbalances exist between participants, requires skilled facilitation.
- Integrating RJ into Existing Legal/Educational Frameworks: Aligning RJ with existing disciplinary codes, legal requirements, and other school initiatives (like PBIS or SEL) can be complex.

- To navigate these challenges and achieve successful, sustainable implementation, several best practices are recommended:
    o Cultivate a Relational Culture: Shift the school's focus from rules and punishment to building and maintaining positive relationships. This requires a fundamental change in mindset among all staff.
    o Develop Staff Mastery through Sustained Professional Development: One-off training sessions are insufficient. Schools must invest in ongoing, high-quality professional development, coaching, and opportunities for staff to practice and reflect on restorative techniques. This builds both skill and commitment.
    o Ensure Equitable Access and Implementation: RJ practices must be applied equitably to all students, guarding against biases that might disproportionately target or exclude certain groups.
    o Empower Sustained Implementation: Secure multi-year funding and administrative support to allow RJ initiatives the time needed to take root and demonstrate impact. Avoid pressure for immediate, unrealistic results.
    o Replace Conflicting Policies: Gradually phase out zero-tolerance policies and other punitive disciplinary frameworks that contradict restorative principles.

- Whole-School Approach: Integrate community-building strategies, interpersonal skill development, and restorative responses into all aspects of school life, rather than treating RJ as an isolated program.
- Center Student and Community Voices: Involve students, families, and community members in the planning, implementation, and evaluation of RJ initiatives to ensure they are relevant and meet local needs.

By addressing these challenges proactively and adhering to best practices, schools can harness the transformative potential of restorative justice to create safer, more supportive, and more equitable learning environments.

Chapter 18: Comprehensive School Mental Health

Recognizing the profound impact of mental health on learning, behavior, and overall well-being, schools are increasingly seen as critical settings for providing mental health support to children and adolescents. A Comprehensive School Mental Health System (CSMHS) moves beyond simply reacting to crises and instead aims to proactively integrate a full continuum of mental health promotion, prevention, early intervention, and treatment services into the fabric of the school environment. This chapter will explore strategies for such integration, the vital roles of specialized school staff, early intervention and prevention approaches, the importance of trauma-informed practices, and models for crisis intervention and post-crisis support.

Integrating Mental Health into the School Fabric

Integrating mental health into the school fabric involves a fundamental shift from viewing mental health services as ancillary to recognizing them as an essential component of education. This holistic approach requires embedding mental health literacy, support, and services into the daily life and culture of the school. The goal is to create an environment where emotional well-being is prioritized alongside academic achievement, and where seeking help for mental health challenges is normalized and destigmatized.

One key concept in this approach is the idea of incorporating age-appropriate mental health education into the curriculum to help students understand mental health concepts, recognize signs of distress in themselves and others, and learn about available resources. This proactive education can empower students and reduce stigma.

Creating a school culture where open conversations about emotions and mental health are encouraged and supported is another important aspect of a supportive climate. This can be facilitated through classroom discussions, school-wide awareness campaigns, and by staff modeling healthy emotional expression.

It's vital that these concepts be extended beyond the student body. All school staff, not just mental health specialists, should receive training to enhance their understanding of child and adolescent mental health, recognize early warning signs of mental health issues, and learn how to provide initial support and make appropriate referrals.

Providing accessible, on-site mental health services, including counseling and support groups, makes it easier for students to receive help in a familiar and less stigmatizing environment. This also removes the barriers of accessing services for students of lesser means or without the desired levels of support at

Because mental health challenges are not contained within the walls of a school, strong collaboration with families and community mental health providers is essential for a comprehensive system. This ensures a coordinated approach to care and allows schools to connect students and families with more intensive services when needed.

Comprehensive School Mental Health Systems (CSMHS) provide a framework for this integration, offering an array of supports that promote positive school climate, social and emotional learning, and overall mental health, while also working to reduce the prevalence and severity of mental illness. These systems typically employ a Multi-Tiered System of Support (MTSS), providing universal mental health promotion for all students (Tier 1), targeted interventions for students at risk (Tier 2), and more intensive treatment for students with significant needs (Tier 3). Technology-enabled services and digital platforms can further support coordination, communication, and data sharing among providers across school and community settings.

By weaving mental health support throughout the school experience, CSMHS aims to create environments where students are more likely to thrive both academically and emotionally.

Roles of School Counselors, Psychologists, and Social Workers

School counselors, psychologists, and social workers, often collectively referred to as Specialized Instructional Support Personnel (SISP), are pivotal figures in the successful implementation of Comprehensive School Mental Health Systems. Their expertise is crucial for prevention, early intervention, assessment, and the provision of direct mental health services to students.

School Social Workers (SSWs), for example, play a multifaceted role. They are essential members of multidisciplinary threat assessment teams, where they help identify appropriate interventions to mitigate risks and reduce the likelihood of students acting on threats. SSWs are skilled in conducting comprehensive bio-psychosocial assessments to gather data that informs interventions or referrals. They can provide specialized treatment for students who have experienced trauma, or those struggling with conflict management and frustration tolerance, and teach anger management techniques. Furthermore, SSWs contribute to the development of 504 plans or Individualized Education Plans (IEPs) for students requiring more intensive academic or special education support, and they actively work to promote school connectedness, a key protective factor against violence.

School counselors and psychologists also contribute significantly by providing individual and group counseling, conducting psychological assessments, developing and implementing prevention programs (for bullying, substance abuse, etc.), and consulting with teachers and parents to support students' academic and emotional development. They are often at the forefront of crisis intervention efforts and play a key role in fostering a positive school climate.

The roles of these professionals are expanding beyond traditional counseling responsibilities to include more active participation in systemic school-wide efforts, such as violence prevention initiatives, threat assessment, crisis response, and fostering a positive school climate. This evolution requires a broader skill set and a more integrated approach to their work within the school system. However, districts face the persistent challenge of sufficient funding to ensure adequate staffing levels and manageable caseloads for these professionals. High student-to-SISP ratios can severely limit their ability to provide proactive and intensive support, often forcing them into primarily reactive roles. The effectiveness of any CSMHS is heavily dependent on having sufficient, well-trained personnel to meet the diverse mental health needs of the student population.

Early Intervention and Prevention Strategies

Early intervention and prevention are critical components of a comprehensive school mental health system, aiming to identify and support students at the first signs of distress or risk, thereby preventing problems from escalating into more severe mental health crises or violent behavior. A proactive approach is generally more effective and less resource-intensive than solely relying on reactive crisis management. Schools can implement a variety of proactive initiatives for early intervention and prevention.

Universal prevention programs are delivered to all students and aim to build protective factors and essential life skills. Social and Emotional Learning (SEL) programs, for instance, teach students skills in areas like emotional regulation, stress management, and interpersonal problem-solving, which can prevent the development of behavioral issues.

For students identified as being at risk or showing early signs of difficulty, targeted interventions can provide additional support. Examples include:

- *The Incredible Years*: This program engages teachers, parents, and young children to reduce disruptive behavior disorders and promote social competence. It has shown robust positive effects in decreasing disruptive behavior and increasing prosocial behavior.
- *Good Behavior Game* (GBG): This classroom-based behavior management program for early elementary students has demonstrated long-lasting positive effects, including significantly lower rates of drug and alcohol use disorders,

antisocial personality disorder, and delinquency in young adulthood for participants. The long-term societal benefits of such early interventions, in terms of reduced costs associated with crime, healthcare, and lost productivity, are substantial.

- *Teacher-Child Interaction Training* (TCIT): A classroom intervention for young children (ages 3-7) that aims to improve positive teacher behavior and classroom environment, leading to improved student resilience and behavioral control.
- *Daily Report Cards* (DRC): An evidence-based behavior modification program for children (ages 6-12) with disruptive behavior disorders, involving collaboration between school and home to address and reward progress on targeted behaviors.
- *Mental Health Screening*: Systematically screening students for mental health concerns can help identify those who may need additional support before problems become more severe. However, screening must be conducted ethically, with appropriate consent, follow-up, and access to services.

Educating students about mental health and destigmatizing seeking help can encourage them to reach out for support when they need it.

A comprehensive approach to school mental health requires both universal strategies to build a healthy foundation for all students and targeted interventions for those who require additional support. Early intervention not only helps prevent the escalation of individual problems but also contributes to a safer and more positive school climate overall.

Trauma-Informed Practices in Schools

Given the high prevalence of trauma among children and adolescents, adopting trauma-informed practices is essential for creating school environments that are safe, supportive, and conducive to learning for all students. Trauma-informed care recognizes the widespread impact of trauma and understands potential paths for recovery; it involves responding by fully integrating knowledge about trauma into policies, procedures, and practices, and seeks to actively resist re-traumatization.

Safety in this context means ensuring physical, emotional, and psychological safety for students and staff. This involves creating predictable routines, clear expectations, and environments free from bullying and harassment. Building trust through clear communication, consistent actions, and transparent decision-making processes are some of the most important steps toward achieving this sense of safety.

It is also vital that students feel they are receiving opportunities for input and decision-making. This inclusion fosters a sense of community and mutual support among students. Encouraging collaboration among students, staff, families, and community partners in creating a trauma-sensitive environment is a challenging, but rewarding, activity.

Chapter 19: Protective Factors and Advocacy

The establishment of safe and nurturing school environments necessitates a comprehensive approach that prioritizes the well-being of students and fosters a sense of community. A critical element of this approach involves enhancing protective factors that mitigate the risk of violence and promoting advocacy to create sustainable change.

The Role of School Connectedness in Safety

A fundamental protective factor against school violence is school connectedness. This concept refers to the belief held by students that the adults and peers within their school community genuinely care about their academic progress and their overall well-being as individuals. This encompasses a student's sense of being cared for, valued, supported, and of belonging to the school environment. Research has consistently shown that when young people feel a strong connection to their school, they are significantly less likely to engage in a range of risky behaviors. These behaviors include substance use, early sexual activity, gang involvement, and, importantly, violence. This strong inverse relationship suggests that cultivating school connectedness can serve as a vital primary prevention strategy, reducing the likelihood of students resorting to harmful actions.

School connectedness holds particular significance for students who are at an elevated risk of experiencing alienation or isolation. This includes students with disabilities, those who identify as lesbian, gay, bisexual, transgender, or are questioning their sexual orientation, students experiencing homelessness, and any student who is chronically truant due to various challenging circumstances. For these vulnerable student populations, a strong sense of belonging and support within the school can act as a crucial buffer against the additional challenges and stressors they may face. Providing them with this protective factor can significantly improve their overall well-being and reduce their vulnerability to negative outcomes.

Implementing strategies to foster school connectedness requires a multifaceted, whole-school approach involving the active participation of various stakeholders. These strategies include creating transparent and inclusive decision-making processes that facilitate the engagement of students, families, and the wider community. Utilizing effective classroom management and teaching methods to cultivate a positive and supportive learning environment is also essential. Furthermore, providing ongoing professional development and support for teachers and other school staff equips them with the necessary skills to meet the diverse cognitive, emotional, and social needs of children and adolescents. At its core, enhancing school connectedness involves nurturing trusting and caring relationships that promote open communication among administrators, teachers, staff, students, families, and the broader community.

Research further indicates that school connectedness can play a critical role in mitigating the negative effects of early adversity on youth. Specifically, it has been shown to buffer against the detrimental impacts of social deprivation in predicting externalizing behaviors and promoting positive functioning. This suggests that the supportive relationships and sense of belonging experienced at school can, to a significant extent, compensate for lower levels of social support in a student's home and neighborhood. This underscores the vital role that schools play in the lives of at-risk youth, offering a protective environment that can counteract the negative influences of challenging circumstances outside of school.

Cultivating a Positive and Supportive School Climate

Beyond individual connectedness, the overall school climate plays a crucial role in fostering safety and preventing violence. A positive school climate is characterized by an environment where the academic, social, emotional, behavioral, and mental health needs of all students are effectively addressed. It reflects the quality and character of school life, indicating how safe, supported, and engaged both students and staff feel within the school setting.

Extensive research has established a strong link between a positive school climate and a range of improved student outcomes. These include higher rates of attendance, improved academic performance as measured by test scores, increased promotion and graduation rates, and a reduced likelihood of students engaging in destructive or violent behaviors. This clear correlation underscores that efforts to cultivate a positive school climate are not merely about improving the general atmosphere but are direct and effective violence prevention strategies. When students feel safe, respected, and supported in their school environment, they are more likely to thrive academically and less inclined to engage in behaviors that could harm themselves or others.

Creating and maintaining a positive school climate involves attention to several key elements. These include ensuring both physical and emotional safety for all members of the school community. Providing a supportive academic setting where students feel encouraged and challenged is also crucial. Clear and fair disciplinary policies that are consistently applied contribute to a sense of justice and order. Fostering respectful, trusting, and caring relationships throughout the school community is paramount. Finally, ensuring access to comprehensive mental health support for students and staff is increasingly recognized as a vital component of a positive school climate.

A positive school climate can also play a significant preventative role in school safety. By fostering an environment where students feel connected and supported, schools can reduce the incidence of behaviors that often contribute to crises, such as violence and bullying. Furthermore, in a positive climate, students are more likely to develop strong relationships with staff and peers, increasing the likelihood that they will quickly report potential threats to trusted adults within the school. This proactive communication is essential for early intervention and can potentially prevent violent incidents from occurring.

Social and emotional learning (SEL) has emerged as a key method for promoting a positive school climate and, consequently, preventing school violence. Integrating SEL into the curriculum and school culture helps to cultivate a more positive and safer environment by equipping students with the skills needed to manage their emotions, build healthy relationships, and make responsible decisions. This interconnectedness of protective factors demonstrates how initiatives focused on enhancing students' social and emotional competencies directly contribute to a more positive and secure school setting.

Integrating Social and Emotional Learning to Build Resilience

Social and Emotional Learning (SEL) is a critical process through which young people develop and apply the knowledge, skills, and attitudes necessary to navigate life effectively. This includes the ability to understand and manage their emotions, set and achieve positive goals, feel and show empathy for others, establish and maintain supportive relationships, and make responsible and caring decisions.

A substantial body of research consistently supports SEL as a highly effective tool for reducing bullying, aggression, and violent behavior within school settings. Numerous meta-analyses, which synthesize the findings from multiple studies, have demonstrated the significant positive effects of SEL programs on various student outcomes. These include improvements in students' social and emotional skills, their attitudes toward themselves and others, their overall behavior, and even their academic performance. The strength and consistency of this evidence base underscore the vital role that SEL plays in a comprehensive strategy for preventing school violence.

SEL programs are designed to build a range of essential skills that directly contribute to a safer school environment. These include the development of empathy, which allows students to understand and share the feelings of others. They foster healthy relationship skills, enabling students to connect with peers and adults in positive ways. SEL also promotes self-control, helping students manage their impulses and reactions. Furthermore, these programs enhance self-advocacy skills, empowering students to express their needs and stand up for themselves and others constructively. Problem-solving and conflict resolution skills are also key components, teaching students how to navigate disagreements peacefully. Finally, SEL cultivates perspective-taking abilities and a deeper understanding of emotions, both in oneself and in others. By developing these core competencies, students are better equipped to navigate social situations constructively and are less likely to resort to violence or bullying.

Studies have shown that schools with actively implemented SEL programs tend to experience lower rates of violence compared to schools that do not prioritize students' social-emotional development. This direct comparison provides tangible evidence of the positive impact of SEL on school safety. The difference in reported violence levels highlights the effectiveness of SEL as a proactive violence prevention strategy.

It is also important to note that culturally responsive SEL programs, which are carefully adapted to the specific cultural contexts and backgrounds of the students they serve, may be even more effective. Tailoring SEL initiatives to meet the diverse needs of the student population enhances their relevance and impact, ensuring that the skills and concepts taught resonate with students from various sociocultural backgrounds.

The Importance of School-Based Mental Health Services

Schools are increasingly recognized as ideal settings for providing mental and behavioral health services to children and adolescents. This is due to their ability to reach a large number of young people and offer opportunities for prevention, early intervention, and the promotion of positive development.

Research indicates a direct link between students' mental health and the safety of the school environment. Students who are experiencing untreated mental health conditions are more likely to exhibit behaviors that can disrupt the school setting, including aggression, withdrawal, and impulsiveness. Addressing these mental health issues early on can significantly reduce the likelihood of these risks escalating into more serious problems. This underscores the necessity of providing accessible mental health support within the school setting as a crucial component of violence prevention.

Comprehensive school-based mental health services should encompass a continuum of support organized across three tiers of intervention. Tier 1 involves universal support for all students, such as mental health literacy programs and the promotion of positive school climate. Tier 2 provides targeted interventions for students identified as being at risk of developing mental health challenges. Tier 3 offers intensive support and services for students with significant mental health needs. Integrating these mental health initiatives with the school's academic programming is essential for gaining the support of administrators and ensuring that mental health support is viewed as integral to the school's primary mission of education. Furthermore, clear methods of communication about mental health programs and initiatives among staff and across different programs are vital for effective implementation.

Implementing the best practices in school-based mental health support is crucial for success. This includes actively engaging school and district leadership in the planning and support of mental health initiatives. It also involves the active participation of families and students in the planning process, ensuring that their perspectives and needs are considered. Building the mental health literacy of all school staff through training and professional development is essential. Finally, utilizing data to inform decision-making and monitor the effectiveness of mental health services is a key component of a robust system.

School mental health programming should offer a comprehensive array of services that address the full spectrum of student needs. This includes primary prevention efforts aimed at promoting overall well-being and preventing the development of mental health conditions. Early intervention services are crucial for identifying and addressing emerging mental health challenges before they escalate. Finally, providing access to treatment services for students with diagnosed mental health conditions is essential for fostering a sense of safety and preventing the worsening of these conditions.

Empowering Students and Fostering Advocacy for a Safer School Environment

Students themselves can be powerful agents of change in creating safer school environments. Actively involving them in peer-led programs that promote positive behaviors, bystander intervention strategies, and anti-bullying campaigns can be highly effective. Providing students with genuine opportunities to have a voice in decision-making processes related to school safety and climate empowers them to become co-creators of inclusive and safe learning spaces.

Establishing anonymous reporting systems within schools can significantly encourage students to report potential problems or concerns to school officials without fear of retaliation. These systems can take various forms, such as online reporting forms, confidential text message lines, or physical drop boxes located in accessible areas of the school. By providing these confidential channels, schools can gain valuable insights into potential threats or issues that students might otherwise be hesitant to share openly.

It is also essential to encourage students to take personal responsibility for maintaining safe school environments and to resist peer pressure that might lead them to act irresponsibly. Fostering this sense of shared responsibility and promoting prosocial norms among the student body can contribute significantly to a more secure and supportive school community. When students feel empowered to make positive choices and understand their role in maintaining safety, it strengthens the overall culture of well-being within the school.

The Role of Positive Relationships with Adults and Peers

Positive relationships with both adults and peers are fundamental to students' overall well-being and contribute significantly to creating a safe and supportive school environment. Research indicates that having a secure relationship with at least one caring adult can act as a buffer against the negative effects of stress and traumatic experiences in a child's life. Furthermore, students who feel a strong sense of school connectedness believe that the adults and their peers at school care about their learning and about them as individuals, fostering a crucial sense of belonging.

Schools that prioritize the development of relationally rich environments can positively influence both the mental health and the learning outcomes of their students. This highlights the synergistic effect of positive relationships, benefiting both students' emotional well-being and their academic success. When students experience strong and supportive connections at school, they are more likely to be engaged in their learning and to report better mental health outcomes.

Educators play a vital role in fostering these positive relationships. Taking the time to learn the names of all students is a simple yet powerful action that can build connections, combat feelings of unimportance, and promote a sense of connectedness and belonging. This seemingly small gesture can reinforce critical feelings of trust, mutual respect, and safety among students.

Chapter 20: Crisis Prevention and Intervention

A proactive approach to school safety requires the development and implementation of comprehensive crisis prevention and intervention strategies. These strategies must address the multifaceted nature of potential crises and prioritize the behavioral health and well-being of students and staff.

Developing Multi-Tiered Systems of Support (MTSS) for Behavioral Health

Many schools and districts utilize Multi-Tiered Systems of Support (MTSS) as a framework for addressing the diverse needs of their students. This framework provides a systematic approach to supporting students' academic, behavioral, mental health, and social-emotional needs through a continuum of evidence-based practices.

The MTSS framework typically involves three tiers of support. Tier 1 encompasses universal support and practices that are implemented school-wide to benefit all students. This might include social-emotional learning curricula, positive behavior interventions, and mental health awareness campaigns.

Tier 2 provides targeted support and interventions for students who are identified as being at risk for developing academic or behavioral difficulties. These interventions are often delivered in small groups and may address specific needs such as social skills deficits or anxiety.

Tier 3 offers intensive and individualized support for students with significant and persistent challenges. This tier may involve individual counseling, specialized academic instruction, or collaboration with community-based mental health providers. This layered approach ensures that all students receive a foundational level of support, with increasingly intensive interventions available for those who require them most.

Effective implementation of MTSS for behavioral health requires a comprehensive and data-informed approach. This includes having well-trained school and district professionals, such as school psychologists, counselors, and social workers, who are equipped to deliver evidence-based interventions. Establishing clear teaming and collaboration structures among school staff, families, and community partners is also essential for effective coordination of support. Resource mapping, which involves identifying and leveraging existing resources within the school and community, helps to ensure that students have access to the services they need.

The selection and implementation of evidence-based practices, which have been shown to be effective through research, are crucial for maximizing positive outcomes. Systematic screening procedures can help to identify students who may be at risk for behavioral health challenges early on. Finally, the ongoing use of data to inform decision-making, monitor student progress, and evaluate the effectiveness of interventions is a key component of a successful MTSS framework.

Integrating mental health initiatives seamlessly with the school's academic programming is vital for enhancing administrator buy-in and ensuring that mental health support is viewed as an integral aspect of the school's overall mission. When school leaders understand that students' mental health directly impacts their ability to learn and succeed academically, they are more likely to prioritize and allocate resources to support mental health initiatives.

Implementing Trauma-Informed Practices in Schools

Recognizing the pervasive impact of trauma on individuals, schools should adopt trauma-informed practices to create safe, supportive, and healing environments. Trauma-informed approaches acknowledge that many students may have experienced adverse events that can affect their behavior, learning, and overall well-being.

A key aspect of becoming a trauma-informed school is to train all personnel to recognize the potential indicators of trauma among students. This includes understanding the various ways in which trauma can manifest in students' behavior, emotions, and academic performance. Once staff are equipped with this knowledge, they can provide appropriate tiered supports that are sensitive to the needs of students who have experienced trauma.

Disciplinary practices within a trauma-informed school should prioritize teaching more appropriate behaviors and utilize restorative approaches rather than relying on exclusionary punishments. Exclusionary practices, such as suspensions and expulsions, can be re-traumatizing for students who have experienced adversity. In contrast, supportive and restorative approaches focus on understanding the underlying causes of behavior, teaching coping skills, and repairing harm, which aligns with the principles of trauma-informed care.

Creating calm and safe spaces within schools is another crucial strategy for supporting students who may have experienced trauma. These spaces can provide students with a non-judgmental environment where they can express their mental health concerns, regulate their emotions, or simply take a break when feeling overwhelmed. Having dedicated mental health rooms or wellness centers within schools, or even designated quiet areas within classrooms, can offer students a refuge when they need it most.

Supportive and Restorative Approaches to Discipline

Shifting away from purely punitive disciplinary measures towards more supportive and restorative approaches is essential for fostering a positive school climate and preventing violence. Supportive discipline focuses on understanding the reasons behind student misbehavior and teaching them the skills they need to make better choices in the future. Restorative practices, on the other hand, aim to address harm that has occurred by bringing together all affected parties to understand the impact of the actions and to collaboratively develop a plan to repair the harm and rebuild relationships.

These approaches represent a fundamental shift in how schools view and respond to student misbehavior. Instead of solely focusing on punishment, they prioritize learning, accountability, and healing, which aligns directly with the emphasis on behavioral health and positive school climate.

Research has increasingly supported the effectiveness of restorative practices in schools. Studies have shown that when implemented effectively, restorative practices can lead to significant reductions in suspensions, student arrests, bullying incidents, and other violent acts. Furthermore, these practices have been linked to improvements in the school's overall climate, increased student connectedness, and even enhanced academic performance.

Successfully adopting restorative justice practices requires a significant transformation in school culture and may necessitate professional development for staff to help them move away from traditional punitive approaches. This shift involves unlearning ingrained practices and perspectives and embracing a new philosophy of discipline that emphasizes relationships and repair. Providing educators with ongoing training and support is crucial for the successful and sustainable implementation of restorative practices.

Early Identification and Intervention for Students at Risk

Proactive school safety measures include establishing systems for the early identification of students who may be at an elevated risk for engaging in violence, experiencing mental health challenges, or struggling with substance abuse. Early identification allows for the provision of timely intervention and support, potentially preventing crises from occurring.

The development and implementation of threat assessment teams and procedures are critical components of early intervention. These teams, typically composed of school administrators, counselors, psychologists, and potentially law enforcement personnel, are responsible for evaluating and responding to potential threats of violence made by students. Having clear protocols for conducting these assessments and implementing appropriate interventions is essential for ensuring the safety of the school community.

Research has shown that intervention programs specifically targeting at-risk students can be effective in reducing the likelihood of acts of violence. These programs may involve individual or group counseling, mentoring, social skills training, or other evidence-based interventions designed to address the specific needs and risk factors of these students. Providing tailored support can help students develop coping mechanisms and make positive choices.

Mental health literacy training for all school staff can significantly enhance early identification efforts. Equipping teachers, administrators, and other school personnel with a basic understanding of mental health challenges, their warning signs, and available resources can increase the likelihood that students in need will be recognized and provided with appropriate support or referrals to mental health professionals.

Effective Crisis Response and Recovery Protocols

Despite proactive prevention efforts, schools must also have well-defined crisis plans and preparedness training in place to effectively respond to emergencies. These plans should outline clear procedures for responding to various types of crises, including violent incidents, natural disasters, and medical emergencies. Regular preparedness drills, involving students and staff, are essential for ensuring that everyone knows what to do in the event of an emergency.

Crisis response protocols should specifically include strategies for mitigating the psychological effects of emergency procedures such as lockdowns. Providing clear and age-appropriate information to students and staff during and after a lockdown can help to reduce anxiety and fear. Protocols should also address the safe and efficient reunification of students with their families following a crisis event.

Crucially, recovery efforts following a crisis must prioritize the provision of emotional and mental health services and support to all members of the school community. Recognizing that even after the immediate danger has passed, students and staff may experience significant emotional distress or trauma, schools must have plans in place to provide access to counseling, support groups, and other mental health resources. This commitment to the long-term well-being of the school community is essential for fostering resilience and promoting healing in the aftermath of a crisis.

Chapter 21: The Role of Technology in Safety

Technology presents both opportunities and challenges in the context of school safety. When used strategically and ethically, it can be a valuable tool for enhancing mental health support, facilitating early warning systems, and promoting a positive school climate. However, it is crucial to be mindful of potential risks related to data privacy and digital citizenship.

Leveraging Technology for Mental Health Support and Resources

Technology can significantly expand access to mental health support and resources for students. Online platforms can provide students with information about mental health conditions, coping strategies, and available services. Mental health apps can offer tools for managing stress, anxiety, and depression. Telehealth services can connect students with mental health professionals remotely, overcoming barriers such as geographical limitations or a reluctance to seek in-person help. This increased accessibility can be particularly beneficial for students in rural areas or those who may feel uncomfortable discussing their mental health concerns face-to-face.

Schools can also utilize technology to enhance mental health literacy within the school community. Online training modules and digital curricula can provide engaging and accessible ways for students and staff to learn about mental health issues, recognize warning signs in themselves and others, and understand how to access support. This can help to reduce stigma associated with mental health challenges and encourage more students to seek help when needed.

Utilizing Technology for Early Warning and Reporting Systems (focused on behavioral indicators)

Anonymous reporting systems, facilitated by technology, can be a valuable tool for early intervention. Online reporting forms accessible through the school website or learning management system, confidential text message lines, or even secure drop boxes accessible via a school app can provide students with a safe and discreet way to report concerns about potential violence, bullying, or other safety issues without fear of retaliation.

While the use of data analytics to identify patterns of concerning online behavior or social media activity could potentially indicate a student in distress or posing a threat, this approach raises significant ethical and privacy concerns. If such technologies are considered, it is crucial to have clear policies and procedures in place that prioritize student privacy, ensure data security, and are transparent with students and families about how their data is being used.

Promoting Digital Citizenship and Preventing Cyberbullying

In today's digitally connected world, it is essential for schools to educate students about responsible online behavior. This includes teaching them about the risks and consequences of cyberbullying, strategies for staying safe online, and the importance of respectful communication in digital spaces. Digital citizenship education equips students with the skills and knowledge to navigate the online world ethically and responsibly.

Schools can also utilize digital resources and tools to monitor and address incidents of cyberbullying. Many platforms offer features that allow students to report cyberbullying, and schools can use software to identify and track online harassment. However, a comprehensive approach to preventing cyberbullying involves not only technological solutions but also educating students about empathy and respect, providing support to victims, and implementing clear policies and consequences for online misconduct.

Ethical Considerations and Data Privacy in Technology Use

The use of technology for school safety purposes must be carefully considered from an ethical standpoint, with a strong emphasis on protecting student data and ensuring compliance with privacy laws. Schools must have clear policies regarding the collection, storage, and use of student data obtained through technology. Transparency with students and families about these policies is crucial for building trust and ensuring accountability.

The Strategic Use of Technology to Enhance Communication and Community Engagement

Technology can be a powerful tool for enhancing communication and fostering community engagement in school safety efforts. School websites, email newsletters, social media platforms, and school-wide communication apps can be used to share information with parents and the wider community about school safety protocols, mental health resources, upcoming events, and opportunities for involvement. This can help to keep the community informed and engaged in creating a safer and more supportive environment for students.

Chapter 22: Community Support for School Safety

Creating safer schools is not solely the responsibility of educators and administrators; it requires active engagement and support of the entire community. This chapter will focus on strategies for building strong partnerships with parents, community organizations, and mental health providers to create a comprehensive network of support for school safety.

Engaging Parents and Families as Key Partners

Parents and families are integral partners in promoting school safety and student well-being. Research consistently demonstrates that parent engagement in schools is linked to a multitude of positive outcomes for students, including improved behavior, higher academic achievement, and a reduced likelihood of engaging in risky behaviors and violence. Studies have specifically found that higher levels of parent involvement in school activities are associated with fewer incidents of school violence, particularly in elementary and middle schools. This underscores the direct protective effect that active parental participation can have on the safety of the school environment.

Furthermore, parent involvement can serve as a particularly important protective factor in schools with a high proportion of racial/ethnic minority students or those located in neighborhoods with high crime rates. This highlights the crucial role that engaged parents can play in mitigating the impact of social and economic inequities on school safety in vulnerable communities.

Schools need to proactively work to build and sustain meaningful parent involvement. This includes actively connecting with parents through various channels, offering a diverse range of opportunities for them to be involved in their children's education and school life, and addressing any common challenges that might hinder their engagement. By fostering strong home-school partnerships, schools can create a more comprehensive and supportive network that benefits student safety and well-being.

Fostering Collaboration with Community Organizations and Mental Health Providers

Addressing the complex issue of school violence effectively requires a collaborative approach that extends beyond the school walls. Schools should actively build partnerships with community-based mental health agencies, social service organizations, and other relevant community groups to provide comprehensive support for students and their families. These collaborative relationships can bring diverse expertise, additional resources, and alternative perspectives to school safety efforts, leading to more effective and multi-faceted prevention strategies.

Addressing Social Determinants of Health and Violence

A comprehensive approach to school violence prevention must also acknowledge and address the broader social and economic factors that can contribute to violence. These social determinants of health include factors such as poverty, inequality, access to quality healthcare, and community violence. These factors can significantly impact students' lives and increase their risk of both perpetrating and experiencing violence. School safety efforts should consider these underlying issues and work to connect students and families with resources and support that address these broader needs.

Creating Safe and Supportive School-Community Partnerships

Building strong relationships and fostering a sense of shared responsibility between schools and the wider community is crucial for creating a safe and supportive environment for students. Active community involvement can provide valuable resources and support for school programs aimed at violence prevention, positive youth development, and mental health promotion. When the community is actively engaged in supporting schools, it reinforces the message that school safety is a collective priority and strengthens the overall safety net for students.

Chapter 23: Behavioral Health-Centered School Safety

To achieve lasting change in school safety, it is essential to advocate for policies that prioritize behavioral health and positive school climate over reliance on armed security measures. This chapter will outline key policy recommendations aimed at creating safer and more supportive school environments.

Challenging Our Reliance on Armed Security Measures

The central premise of this book is that armed security measures do not enhance school safety and may, in fact, create a climate of fear and distrust, potentially making schools less safe. Policies should instead prioritize proactive, preventative strategies that address the root causes of violence by focusing on mental health support, social-emotional learning, positive school climate initiatives, and restorative justice practices. Investing in school counselors, psychologists, and social workers, as well as evidence-based prevention programs, is a more effective and sustainable approach to creating safe and nurturing learning environments.

Promoting Policies that Prioritize Mental Health and School Climate

Advocacy efforts should focus on promoting policies that mandate and adequately fund comprehensive school-based mental health services. This includes ensuring access to universal mental health screening, prevention programs, early intervention services for students showing signs of distress, and treatment options for those with diagnosed mental health conditions. Policies should also support the widespread implementation of evidence-based Social and Emotional Learning (SEL) programs in all schools, recognizing their proven effectiveness in reducing violence and promoting positive student outcomes. Furthermore, policies should encourage and support initiatives that foster a positive and supportive school climate characterized by strong student connectedness, a sense of safety and belonging, and high levels of student engagement.

Advocating for Increased Funding for School-Based Mental Health Services and SEL Programs

To effectively implement these behavioral health-centered policies, it is crucial to advocate for increased state and federal funding to support school-based mental health services and SEL programs. Research has consistently demonstrated the cost-effectiveness and long-term benefits of these interventions. Policymakers need to understand that investing in the behavioral health and well-being of students is a wise investment that yields significant returns in terms of improved school safety, academic outcomes, and overall societal well-being.

Policy Recommendations for Restorative Justice and Supportive Discipline

Finally, advocacy efforts should promote policies that encourage or mandate the adoption of restorative justice practices and other supportive discipline approaches in schools. These policies should aim to replace ineffective zero-tolerance policies that have been shown to disproportionately impact marginalized students and fail to address the underlying causes of misbehavior. Restorative justice offers a more constructive and relationship-centered approach to discipline that focuses on repairing harm and fostering accountability.

Chapter 24: A Culture of Safety and Well-being

Achieving lasting school safety requires a commitment to creating a sustainable culture of safety and well-being that is deeply embedded in the fabric of the school community. This chapter will explore the systemic changes, professional development initiatives, and ongoing evaluation processes necessary to achieve this goal.

Implementing System-Wide Changes in School Culture and Practices

Creating a sustainable culture of safety and well-being necessitates a fundamental shift in school culture and practices. This involves prioritizing student well-being, social-emotional development, and positive relationships as foundational elements of a safe and thriving learning environment. This shift requires a commitment from all stakeholders – students, staff, families, and the wider community – to embrace a shared vision of a supportive and nurturing school climate.

Professional Development for Educators on Behavioral Health and Trauma-Informed Care

Ongoing and comprehensive professional development for all school staff is essential for sustaining a focus on behavioral health and well-being. This training should cover topics such as recognizing and responding to student mental health needs, implementing trauma-informed practices, utilizing restorative justice techniques, and integrating social-emotional learning into the curriculum and classroom management strategies. Equipping educators with knowledge and skills in these areas is crucial for fostering a supportive and safe school environment.

Continuous Monitoring and Evaluation of School Safety Initiatives

To ensure the effectiveness and sustainability of school safety initiatives, it is vital to establish systems for continuous monitoring and evaluation. Schools should regularly collect and analyze data on key indicators such as school climate, student behavior, bullying incidents, and the utilization of mental health services. This data can then be used to assess the impact of implemented programs, identify areas for improvement, and ensure accountability in achieving school safety goals.

Building Leadership Capacity for Sustainable Change

Strong leadership at both the school and district levels is critical for championing and supporting a culture of safety and well-being. Leaders play a vital role in setting the vision, allocating resources, and ensuring that policies and practices align with the goal of creating a safe, supportive, and nurturing environment for all students. Building leadership capacity in this area will help to ensure the long-term sustainability of school safety efforts.

Chapter 25: Sustainable Financial Strategies

Implementing a comprehensive, holistic approach to school safety requires a significant and sustained investment in personnel, programs, training, and partnerships. While the long-term benefits in terms of improved student outcomes and reduced societal costs are substantial, securing adequate and flexible funding can be a major challenge for schools and districts. This chapter explores various funding streams—federal, state, local, and grant-based—and discusses how "braided funding" models can be strategically employed to support and sustain these vital initiatives.

(Unfortunately, I need to include an important disclaimer here: the current GOP-led federal administration and congress are, at the time of this writing, working shutter the Department of Education, defund Medicaid, and have appointed uniquely unqualified and dangerous individuals to lead the Departments of Education and Health and Human Services. These departments would under normal circumstances represent the primary sources of funding and policy support that I advocate for in this book. I have considered removing this section from the text but chose to leave this information as an illustration of the popularly overlooked ways in which the federal government, under normal circumstances, helps states address challenges of this kind.)

Exploring Funding Streams: Federal, State, Local, and Grant Opportunities

A diverse array of funding sources can potentially be tapped to support different components of a holistic school safety model. Navigating this landscape requires proactive research, strategic planning, and often dedicated grant-writing capacity.

- Federal Funding:
    - Department of Education:
        - Elementary and Secondary School Emergency Relief (ESSER) Fund: Part of COVID-19 relief packages (like the American Rescue Plan Act), these funds have provided significant, albeit temporary, resources that many states and districts have used for mental health services, SEL programs, and other supports to address pandemic impacts.
        - Bipartisan Safer Communities Act (BSCA): This act allocated substantial new funding for school-based mental health services and professionals, as well as for school safety programs.
        - Title IV, Part A (Student Support and Academic Enrichment Grants): These grants can be used for a wide range of activities, including those that support safe and healthy students (e.g., mental health services, drug and violence prevention, SEL) and provide a well-rounded education.

- School Climate Transformation Grants: Competitive grants for SEAs and LEAs to implement multi-tiered behavioral frameworks.
- Individuals with Disabilities Education Act (IDEA): Funds can be used to provide mental health services for students with disabilities as part of their Individualized Education Programs (IEPs).
  - Department of Health and Human Services (HHS) and SAMHSA:
    - Project AWARE (Advancing Wellness and Resilience in Education): Grants to states and districts to increase mental health awareness, train school personnel, and connect youth to services.
    - Mental Health Block Grants: Allocated to states, which can then distribute funds for various mental health initiatives, potentially including school-based services.
    - Other Project Grants: SAMHSA offers various discretionary grants that may support specific aspects of school mental health or substance abuse prevention.
  - Department of Justice (DOJ):

- STOP School Violence Act Program: Grants to states, LEAs, and tribal organizations to improve school security, support school threat assessment and crisis intervention teams, and provide training.
  - Medicaid: A key source of funding for school-based health and mental health services for eligible students. Schools can receive reimbursement for medically necessary services, including those outlined in IEPs, and for some administrative activities related to connecting students to Medicaid services.
- State Funding:
  - General Education Formulas and Categorical Aid: Some states incorporate funding for counselors, social workers, or safety initiatives directly into their school funding formulas or provide specific categorical aid for these purposes.
  - State-Specific Grant Programs: Many states offer competitive grants for school safety, mental health, SEL, or violence prevention initiatives. For example, New York has specific funding for school-based mental health clinics, and California has major initiatives like the Community Schools Partnership Program and the Children and Youth Behavioral Health Initiative.

- Legislative Earmarks/Line Items: State budgets may include specific line-item appropriations for school mental health resource centers or other safety-related projects.
    - Special Revenue (e.g., Proposition 301 in Arizona): Dedicated revenue streams from taxes or propositions can be allocated to school safety programs.
- Local Funding:
    - School District General Funds: A significant portion of school safety and mental health expenses often comes from local school district budgets, derived from property taxes and other local revenue.
    - Municipal Budgets/City Taxes: In some cases, city or county funds may contribute to school-based programs, particularly those involving partnerships with local agencies.
- Grants and Private Foundations:
    - Private Foundations: Numerous national and local foundations provide grants for education, youth development, mental health, and violence prevention initiatives that can align with holistic school safety goals.
    - Corporate Sponsorships: Some businesses may partner with schools or districts to support specific programs or provide resources.

The challenge for schools and districts lies in identifying these diverse opportunities, understanding their specific requirements and allowable uses, and strategically aligning them with their comprehensive safety plans. This often requires dedicated staff time for research, grant writing, and program management.

Braided Funding Models for Comprehensive Services

Given that no single funding stream is likely to cover all aspects of a holistic school safety model, and many grants are time-limited and match-limited, braided funding has emerged as a crucial strategy for sustainability and comprehensiveness. Braided funding involves coordinating multiple funding sources (federal, state, local, private) to support a unified program or set of services, while keeping the accounting for each funding stream separate to meet individual reporting requirements. This is distinct from blended funding, where funds are comingled into a single pool with unified requirements, which is often more difficult to achieve due to differing statutory and regulatory constraints, and the specific requirements associated with grant funding.

Braided funding models have many tangible benefits. They allow schools to layer different funding sources to cover a wider range of services and activities than any single source could support alone. They enable support of multi-component programs that address various facets of holistic safety. This method also serves as a way of promoting program sustainability; braided funding diversifies revenue streams, reducing reliance on any single grant or appropriation that might be temporary or subject to change, thereby minimizing potential losses if one source of dollars goes dry.

Because funding initiatives often require and encourage partnerships between different agencies and organizations (education, health, mental health) as they work together to coordinate services and funding, there are challenges to this model.

Managing multiple funding streams with different eligibility criteria, allowable uses, reporting requirements, and timelines can be administratively burdensome, requiring specialized training and staffing. Funds from specific sources can often only be used within a strictly designated scope, limiting flexibility and requiring regular scrutiny of spending.

These challenges can be overcome with intentional planning and proper oversight. Clearly identifying the goals, specific services needed, and target populations to guide the search for appropriate funding sources is vital.

The planning should identify all potential federal, state, local, and private funding streams relevant to the different components of the holistic safety plan. Once identified, it is important to establish clear agreements with partner agencies regarding roles, responsibilities, service delivery, and how and by whom different funding streams will be coordinated.

Consideration should be made to have dedicated staff, whether as a district employee or by contracting with an administrative organization, to manage contracts, track fund utilization across different streams, and handle reporting requirements. This also includes advocating with funders and policymakers for greater flexibility in how funds can be used and for streamlined reporting requirements where possible.

Clearly articulating the intended outcomes of the program and developing a plan for evaluating its impact are crucial for securing and sustaining funding.

There are many examples of braided funding in action. For instance, Pennsylvania's Student Assistance Program (SAP) utilizes education system funds for training SAP teams and mental health/drug and alcohol allocations from counties to provide liaison services to these teams.

School-based behavioral health or medical programs often rely on a mix of fee-for-service reimbursement (Medicaid, private insurance), district funds, city/county taxes, and grants from private foundations to maintain operating expenses.

The Office of Superintendent of Public Instruction (OSPI) of Washington state notes that the Every Student Succeeds Act (ESSA) provides flexibility for districts to braid federal and state program funds to address local goals, including SEL.

Promise Neighborhoods, a program of the federal government, requires grantees to secure substantial matching funds from private and other government sources, which are then braided to support "cradle-to-career" continuums of services.

While administratively demanding, braided funding offers a viable path toward building more comprehensive and sustainable holistic school safety systems. It requires a shift from chasing individual grants to a long-term model based on strategically designed portfolios of resources aligned with a clear vision and commitment to student well-being.

Successfully funding holistic school safety requires creativity, persistence, and a collaborative spirit. By strategically combining resources, schools and districts can build the comprehensive systems of support that all students deserve to feel safe, nurtured, and ready to learn.

Chapter 26: Holistic School Safety in Your Community

The journey toward creating schools that are truly safe, supportive, and nurturing for every child is a collective endeavor. It requires the active engagement and advocacy of parents, educators, students, community leaders, and policymakers. We have so far seen evidence and strategies for holistic school safety, and I hope this chapter serves as a call to action. By offering concrete ways for different stakeholders to contribute to this transformation in their own communities and beyond, I hope to empower folks at every level to engage where they are able.

Strategies for Parents, Educators, and Community Leaders

Each group possesses unique perspectives, skills, and spheres of influence that can be leveraged to advocate for and implement holistic school safety models. While nature abhors a vacuum, it also rewards diversity. That diversity includes the diverse experiences, thoughts, and attitudes of every community member.

For parents and caregivers, it is vital that we educate ourselves about holistic school safety principles and our school's current safety plans and climate initiatives. Ask school administrators and board members specific questions about mental health support, SEL programs, restorative discipline practices, and how they are creating a positive school climate. Inquire about how physical security measures are balanced with the need to maintain a welcoming environment, and demand that physical security measures (including the presence of SROs) be evaluated and reconsidered at regular intervals. No security measures should be implemented and forgotten; there must be accountability and opportunity for revision.

If we are able, we should participate in PTA/PTO meetings, school safety committees (if they exist, or advocate for their creation with parent representation), and informational sessions. If you are so inclined, run for office in your district. Share your perspectives and personal stories about why holistic safety is important. Volunteer for safety-related tasks if possible.

Importantly, we must maintain open conversations with our children about their experiences at school, their feelings on safety and the drills they experience, and any other concerns they may have. We can reinforce safety awareness and positive coping skills at home, regardless of the policies in place locally.

There are also ways we can advocate directly to policymakers. We can use resources like the National PTA's blueprint to engage with local and state legislators about the need for policies and funding that support comprehensive school safety, including mental health services and restorative justice. Importantly, we must be aware of access to firearms in our homes and the homes our children visit, and throughout the community, and advocate for safe gun storage practices.

For those of us who work in schools, whether as administrators, teachers, counselors, or in other roles, we can advocate within our schools and districts for the adoption and implementation of evidence-based holistic safety strategies, such as SEL, trauma-informed care, and restorative practices.

We can visibly and vocally prioritize building strong, trusting relationships with students and colleagues, as this is foundational to a safe and supportive climate. We must actively seek out and engage in training on holistic safety topics to enhance our skills and knowledge.

To achieve sustainable climates, we must work collaboratively with colleagues across disciplines to support student well-being and share best practices. No school professional can serve the needs of students by operating in a professional silo; we should encourage team communication between staff so that support can be consistent and not become contradictory.

We can participate in or help form school safety and climate teams. We can create opportunities for students and families to share their perspectives and contribute to school improvement efforts, and we can work with our local and national unions or professional associations (like the NEA or AFT) to advocate for policies and contract language that support holistic safety and staff well-being.

If we are fortunate enough to be considered leaders in our communities, whether through elected office, non-profit participation, business ownership, faith organizations, or other avenues, we can use these positions to raise awareness about the importance of comprehensive school safety and advocate for local policies and resource allocation that support it.

We can use these positions to negotiate and support partnerships between schools and community organizations (mental health providers, youth development programs, businesses) to provide integrated services and support for students and families.

We can advocate for local, state, and federal funding for school-based mental health, SEL, and other holistic safety components. And we can explore opportunities for community foundations or businesses to contribute to the positive climate of the community.

Through our public involvement, we must help shape a narrative that moves beyond fear-based reactions to school safety and promotes a more comprehensive, supportive vision. Just the simple act of breaking the taboo on speaking about controversial topics can have a powerful and lasting impact.

Change is most likely to occur when these diverse groups find common ground and work in concert. Parents bring the urgency of their children's well-being, educators offer professional expertise, and community leaders can mobilize broader resources and political will. Together, they can create a powerful force for transforming school environments.

Building Coalitions and Mobilizing for Change

Advocating for systemic change in school safety requires more than individual efforts; it necessitates building broad-based coalitions that can amplify voices, share resources, and sustain pressure for reform. Entrenched systems and mindsets, such as the cultural norm of overreliance on punitive discipline and physical security, can be resistant to change. Overcoming this inertia requires organized, strategic, and sustained, passionate advocacy.

Bringing together diverse stakeholders—parents, students, teachers, counselors, administrators, mental health professionals, community organizations, and sympathetic policymakers—around a shared vision for holistic school safety is important work. Focusing on common values like student well-being, equity, and the desire for thriving schools builds a message that can resonate across entire communities.

It is important to craft clear, concise, and evidence-based messages that articulate the problems with current approaches and the benefits of holistic safety. When we tailor messages to resonate with different audiences (emphasizing student outcomes for educators, cost-effectiveness for policymakers, child well-being for parents), we can be more successful in garnering support. It's important to reinforce interconnectedness and the positive effects of safe schools on the wider community.

Raising awareness through shared research, data, and personal stories can educate the broader community and policymakers about the need for change. These messages should be disseminated through multiple channels, including community forums, school board meetings, local media, and social media.

Strategic engagement with policymakers can help us understand the policy landscape, which is often more complex than simply convincing someone to agree with us. If we can identify key decision-makers (school board members, superintendents, state legislators, federal representatives) and understand current policies and budget processes, establish ongoing relationships with policymakers and their staff, and provide them with credible information, we are far more likely to drive meaningful policy change. If possible, we can offer to be a resource.

Casting wide nets may be useful, but focusing advocacy efforts on specific policy changes, funding requests, or legislative initiatives that align with holistic safety goals is likely to be more direct and immediately impactful.

Every resident has the ability and the right to participate in public hearings, submit written testimony, and provide input during policy development processes. We can engage and empower a wide base of supporters through petitions, letter-writing campaigns, community meetings, and voter education efforts. Organizations like the Sandy Hook Promise and the National PTA provide tools and platforms for such grassroots action.

There are many examples of schools and districts that have successfully implemented various components of holistic safety – share them to demonstrate that change is possible and beneficial.

Systemic change takes time and effort. Coalitions of any community must be prepared for a long-term commitment and be willing to adapt strategies as needed based on shifting perceptions. Celebrating incremental victories along the way can keep morale high even when the obstacles seem immense.

The National Education Association (NEA) and the American Federation of Teachers (AFT) are examples of large organizations that advocate for policies supporting educator well-being and student-centered approaches to safety, including restorative justice and increased mental health supports. Partnering with or drawing inspiration from such established advocacy groups can be beneficial.

The following table offers actionable recommendations tailored to key stakeholder groups, providing a starting point for engagement.

By working together, these stakeholders can help shift the narrative and the reality of school safety, moving towards a future where every school is a place of genuine security, support, and opportunity for all.

Building Schools Where Every Child is Safe, Supported, and Ready to Learn

The pursuit of safe schools, in my view, is a fundamental obligation we owe to our children. However, the path to achieving this goal must be paved with more than just heightened security measures and punitive responses. As I have argued, true and lasting school safety is only achievable when approached from a holistic approach—one that nurtures the whole child, cultivates a positive and inclusive school climate, empowers all staff, engages families and communities as partners, and actively listens to the voices of students themselves.

The evidence overwhelmingly suggests that our current, myopic reliance on armed security and zero-tolerance policies falls short of popularly expected outcomes. These policies, in fact, create environments of fear, mistrust, and inequity, particularly for students already pushed to the margins. These measures provide only the *appearance* of safety in a world dominated by fear. Reactive and punitive policies address the symptoms of existing distress and conflict, but they are fully unfit to tackle the root causes or offer preventive solutions. In contrast, holistic strategies aim to create conditions where all students feel physically, emotionally, and psychologically secure. Rather than reacting to violence, holistic safety is intended to prevent the radicalization that grows from distress and conflict in inadequately stable or supportive environments.

The journey towards holistic school safety is not a simple one, nor is it a destination that can be reached with a single program or policy. It requires a fundamental shift in mindset, a commitment to continuous improvement, and a willingness to confront popular yet ineffective policies while investing in the long-term well-being of our school communities. It demands that we see safety not as a separate silo, but as inextricably linked to academic achievement, equity, and the overall health of our society.

The path forward involves investing in proactive measures like SEL, behavioral health literacy, and trauma-informed care that equip students with coping skills and address challenges before they escalate; recognizing that strong, trusting relationships among students, staff, and families are the bedrock of a safe and supportive school; moving beyond archaic punitive discipline to modern, person-first practices that focus on repairing harm, prioritizing accountability, and strengthening community bonds.

Moving the holistic safety vision forward also means ensuring that teachers are supported, parents are engaged as partners, community resources are leveraged, and student voices are incorporated into decision-making; continuously examining policies and practices to ensure they are fair, just, and supportive of all students, particularly those who have been historically marginalized; advocating for the financial resources and legislative frameworks necessary to implement and sustain comprehensive, holistic safety initiatives.

Creating schools where every child is safe, supported, and ready to learn is an ambitious goal, but I believe it is an achievable one. It requires collective courage to challenge outdated paradigms, collective wisdom to embrace evidence-based practices, and a collective commitment to action. By working together, parents, educators, policymakers, and community members can transform our schools into the nurturing, empowering, and truly safe growth environments our children deserve. The future well-being of our students, and therefore our communities, depends on it.

Part III: Protection Through Connection

Chapter 27: The Converging Crises

Today's youth navigate a complex terrain marked by multifaceted pressures that can significantly impact their development and well-being. Adolescents today live in a world far more connected and complex than that in which I was raised. This Connected Generation faces challenges that my peers and I could never have dreamed of while attending primary school in the 1980s and 1990s. Young people today are unable to escape the influence of their peers, and yet are some of the most isolated individuals imaginable.

They have grown up never knowing a world without the internet or smartphones, and an entire generation of young people entered the social sphere for the first time following an extended lockdown during which they were unable to form the neurological foundation of personal connection.

Schools have been armored fortresses first, places of learning second, and their schools have been under constant threats to funding and decreasing investment in creative disciplines. In addition to these new challenges, the prevalence of school violence remains a persistent and deeply concerning issue, manifesting not merely as isolated incidents but often as a symptom of broader societal strains and individual vulnerabilities.

To bridge the gaps of development and inclusion created within this confusion of challenges, active fostering of interpersonal and intergenerational relationships can be of extraordinary benefit.

The threat of youth radicalization towards violence presents an inescapable layer of risk, whereby young people, often seeking identity, belonging, or solutions to perceived injustices, can be drawn into extremist ideologies that advocate violence as a legitimate means to an end. These challenges are not uniform in their impact, often disproportionately affecting youth already marginalized by socio-economic factors, lack of supportive networks, or pre-existing mental health conditions. Understanding this landscape is crucial for developing effective preventative strategies, as it underscores the need for interventions that address not just overt behaviors but also the underlying vulnerabilities that can lead young people down destructive paths. The urgency to address these issues is compounded by their potential to derail healthy development, undermine community safety, and perpetuate cycles of violence and alienation.

The Unacknowledged Impact of the Pandemic

The COVID-19 pandemic that began in 2020, and its associated public health measures—lockdowns, school closures, and prolonged social distancing—have profoundly amplified pre-existing vulnerabilities among young people, creating a new layer of challenges that intersect with concerns about violence and radicalization. The pandemic necessitated social isolation, which, while crucial for public health, created additional harm for some youth already at-risk regarding behavior health challenges. This isolation has been linked to lower self-esteem, increased depressive symptoms, abuse, and suicide, all of which are significant risk factors that can heighten susceptibility to negative influences, including extremist ideologies that prey on vulnerable individuals.

Adults who were working with young people during the early stages of the pandemic reported significant concerns regarding mental health, school performance, financial strain, and access to regular, nutritious food. These widespread stressors illustrate the breadth of the crisis faced by young people, potentially making them more receptive to groups or ideologies that offer even a false sense of community, purpose, or seem to provide easy solutions to their distress.

The disruption to education, routine, and social interaction, coupled with heightened anxiety and economic uncertainty within families, has had a demonstrable negative impact on youth behavioral health globally. This environment, characterized by increased isolation and psychological distress, has become a fertile ground for various negative outcomes. For instance, young people spending more time online due to lockdowns might have increased exposure to extremist and radicalizing content, while simultaneously lacking the in-person social support that would normally provide a buffer against such influences. The pandemic's aftermath continues to be felt, with many young people struggling to readjust and cope with the accumulated stress and developmental disruptions, underscoring the need for robust support systems.

The stressors confronting youth—school violence, the risk of radicalization, and the profound impacts of the pandemic—are not isolated phenomena but are often interconnected, creating a complex web of risk factors. The social isolation imposed by the pandemic, for example, may have inadvertently made online radicalization more appealing as young individuals sought connection and belonging in digital spaces.

With traditional social avenues curtailed, the internet became an even more central space for interaction, which, while offering many benefits, also increased exposure to potentially harmful content, including extremist narratives designed to exploit feelings of loneliness and disenfranchisement. This environment saw the rise of extremist social influencers who sell the perception of strength in what has now been termed the "Manosphere" – influencers like Andrew Tate, Joe Rogan, and others have gained reach and power beyond what would have been possible in a world without the lockdown. This suggests a critical consideration for interventions: addressing post-pandemic isolation must also involve strategies to mitigate the risks of increased exposure to, and the skills to resist, harmful online influences.

Furthermore, for some young people, engagement with extremist ideologies or violent behaviors might be understood as a maladaptive response to feelings of overwhelm, stress, a perceived lack of opportunity, or an unsettled search for identity—all issues significantly amplified by the disruptive reality of a deadly pandemic. Extremist groups are effective in crafting narratives that seem to provide a sense of personal significance, purpose, and a clear-cut identity to marginalized or isolated individuals.

Consequently, for youth experiencing heightened psychological distress and a diminished sense of self or hope for the future in the aftermath of COVID, extremist ideologies might present a dangerously appealing, albeit destructive, way of regaining a sense of personal control and coping with negative emotions. This highlights the profound need for interventions, such as mentoring, that can offer healthy coping mechanisms, positive identity development, and a constructive sense of purpose, thereby directly countering these harmful lures.

Chapter 28: The Protective Power of Mentoring

Mentorship, in its many forms, has been identified as a significant protective factor capable of buffering youth against a range of risks, including violence and radicalization. Its power lies primarily in the development of strong, positive relationships that can foster resilience and promote healthy developmental trajectories.

Peer-to-Peer and Adult-Child Dyads

Mentoring establishes a developmental relationship where a more experienced or knowledgeable individual (the mentor) guides and supports a less experienced individual (the mentee). In this chapter, I will focus on two primary models prevalent in school and community settings: adult-child mentoring and peer-to-peer mentoring.

Adult-child mentoring is the most common form and involves a young person, typically under the age of 18, being matched with an adult mentor. These mentors are usually unrelated adults who volunteer their time to provide guidance, support, and encouragement. The premise is that a consistent, caring adult can offer a unique perspective, life experience, and access to resources that can benefit the young person's development.

Peer-to-peer mentoring, sometimes referred to as cross-age peer mentoring, involves participants of similar ages, or slightly older peers, taking on the role of mentor for younger individuals. While less extensively researched than adult-child models, peer mentoring leverages the relatability and shared experiences of individuals closer in age. Student-led clubs focusing on violence prevention, for example, often incorporate elements of peer education and support. The role model in such relationships might be a peer of similar age or background, or someone with slightly more experience or skills.

Regardless of the specific configuration, whether an adult guiding a child or an older peer supporting a younger one, the fundamental aim of these mentoring relationships is to provide consistent support, constructive guidance, and positive role modeling, fostering an environment where the mentee can thrive.

How Mentoring Protects Against Risk

Mentoring produces its protective influence through several interconnected mechanisms, primarily centered on the quality of the mentor-mentee relationship. This supportive, trusting bond in and of itself can act as a significant protective factor against many risks. Evidence suggests that mentored youth are less likely to engage in many disruptive or dangerous behaviors, including violence; for instance, a study of the Big Brothers Big Sisters program found that mentored youth were 33 percent less likely to have hit someone compared to unmentored youth. There are several key mechanisms through which mentoring offers protection.

Mentors act as consistent, positive examples, demonstrating constructive ways of dealing with challenges and interacting with others. This can directly counter the influence of negative role models or antisocial peer groups, including extremists.

A crucial component of effective mentoring is emotional support, which has been linked to stronger positive effects in reducing aggression and delinquency. The mentor provides a safe space for youth to express feelings and concerns. Particularly for young people without a strong support system at home, an emotionally supportive, non-judgmental, unrelated adult can have a remarkably positive impact.

Mentoring relationships enhance a young person's network of social support and facilitate bonding with prosocial adults and organizations, which is associated with reductions in self-reported violent behaviors.

Mentors can guide youth in thinking through consequences and making better choices during challenging developmental periods where executive functioning has not yet been established. Alumni of mentoring programs often report that their mentors helped them make better decisions throughout their childhood and continue to be impactful into adulthood.

Prosocial values are often lacking in youth who are drawn to radicalization or extremist groups. Mentors can help instill an understanding of right and wrong and the importance of empathy and respect for others. By supporting youth through challenges and celebrating successes, mentors help build resilience, enabling mentees to cope more effectively with adversity.

The mentor-mentee relationship itself is key to intervention effectiveness and can directly mitigate "pull factors" such as the need for belonging or a stable identity, which are often exploited by extremist groups. A single, strong, positive relation can create powerful resistance against the aspects of such groups that are so attractive to those who feel isolated and unsupported.

Many protective factors identified in the prevention of general youth violence—such as positive adult relationships, self-control, good school achievement, association with nondeviant peers, and a basic acceptance of societal institutions—are also associated with preventing radicalization. Mentoring can directly contribute to fostering several of these protective factors or help compensate where they are deficient in a young person's environment.

The Significance of Positive Role Models and Secure Attachments

The availability of a positive role model is a cornerstone of healthy youth development. Mentors often fill this crucial role, particularly for young people who may lack consistent, strong parental support or other positive adult figures in their lives. A non-relative adult can provide support similar to that of a parent, including vital emotional support, advice, and guidance, especially when such support from parents is insufficient or absent. In contexts where youth are at risk of gang involvement, credible messengers who have navigated similar past experiences can serve as powerful resistant role models, demonstrating that alternative, constructive paths are possible, a dynamic that works equally well in the prevention of other radicalizations.

The concept of secure attachment, typically formed with primary caregivers, provides a foundation of safety and stability crucial for emotional and social development. While a mentoring relationship is different from a caregiving bond, a strong, consistent, and caring mentor can foster a sense of security and trust that mirrors some aspects of secure attachment. This "earned security" can be particularly important for youth who have experienced insecure or disrupted attachments earlier in life. Such a relationship can provide an emotional anchor, helping young people navigate adolescence with greater confidence and making them less vulnerable to negative influences that promise belonging or validation.

The support offered by mentors is not merely additive; it can actively compensate for significant deficits in a young person's existing support systems. For many at risk youth, a common underlying factor is the absence of consistent, positive adult guidance and strong role models. Mentoring directly addresses this gap by providing formal, structured support in lieu of the support that a caregiver will not or cannot provide. Youth facing significant environmental risk factors, such as those associated with low family income, often discover even greater benefits from mentoring interventions. These factors show how mentoring serves a critical compensatory function by filling a potential void, offering guidance, emotional support, and positive behavioral examples that might otherwise be missing, and directly mitigating risks associated with a lack of important and foundational support.

At its heart, the effectiveness of mentoring resides in the *relationship* itself. It is more than a simple transfer of advice; it is the consistent, caring connection that cultivates trust and opens the door for positive influence. In practice, it is the mentor–mentee relationship itself that is the preventative intervention. Mentoring programs that prioritize emotional support as a core component tend to demonstrate the strongest positive effects. Factors such as frequent, regular interaction, the duration of the mentor-mentee relationship, and the level of trust with a mentor have been associated with stronger academic and behavioral outcomes. This implies that the very process of building and nurturing a high-quality relationship is the primary vehicle through which protective factors are established, and risk factors are minimized. Consequently, the design and implementation of mentoring programs must prioritize the cultivation and sustenance of these meaningful connections.

Radicalization toward violence is a process whereby individuals adopt ideologies that justify the use of violence to achieve specific goals. The skills and attitudes fostered by mentoring to prevent general youth violence, such as empathy, non-violent conflict resolution, and reduced aggression, are directly transferable and highly relevant to the prevention of radicalization in other areas. By strengthening these general protective attributes and diminishing aggressive tendencies, mentoring builds foundational resilience. This makes young people less likely to embrace violent extremist ideologies or engage in violent actions, irrespective of ideological motivation, effectively inoculating them against any specific, ideologically driven form of violence.

Chapter 29: Personal and Professional Growth

Mentoring relationships, while primarily aimed at supporting youth, offer a wealth of benefits that extend to the mentors themselves and contribute to the broader social fabric by building valuable social capital. This reciprocal nature enhances the appeal and sustainability of mentoring initiatives.

Young people engaged in quality mentoring relationships experience a wide array of positive developmental outcomes that span social, emotional, behavioral, and academic domains.

One cornerstone of mentoring's impact is the enhancement of a young person's self-worth. Mentorship provides youth with a sounding board for new ideas or questions, but simply the presence of someone who believes in them is fundamental to building self-esteem and resilience. Personalized support, positive reinforcement, the experience of being listened to and valued, and the achievement of goals within the mentoring context all contribute to increased confidence.

Mentors model and encourage the development of crucial social and emotional competencies. This modeling should be intentional and includes fostering empathy through active listening and exposure to diverse perspectives which can lead to improved social skills overall. Mentees learn to manage their emotions more effectively and build healthier interpersonal relationships.

Mentoring is consistently linked to positive educational outcomes, with reduced absenteeism and improved academic success. Mentored youth tend to have fewer unexcused school absences, develop more positive attitudes toward school, and may even exhibit higher educational aspirations; the introduction of the concept of achievement is sometimes enough to change a student's view of their own potential. Some studies also indicate modest gains in academic performance.

One of the most significant impacts of mentoring is the reduction of engagement in risky and negative behaviors. Overwhelming evidence demonstrates that mentored youth are less likely to become involved with drug and alcohol use, exhibit aggressive behaviors, or be involved in delinquent activities. For example, a 2022 study reported a 21.1 percent reduction in violent behavior and a 14.2 percent reduction in youth offending among mentored youth.

Mentors guide young people in developing critical thinking skills related to personal choices, particularly during the adolescent phases of development where executive functioning is challenging. Alumni of Big Brothers Big Sisters reported that their mentors helped them make better choices. The process of setting and achieving goals with a mentor's support not only builds self-esteem but also enhances practical life skills.

These benefits collectively contribute to a more holistic and positive developmental trajectory for young people with mentors, equipping them with the skills, confidence, and support needed to navigate challenges and pursue their potential.

A Reciprocal Opportunity

The mentoring experience is not a unidirectional flow of benefits; mentors themselves benefit from significant personal and professional development. Recognizing and promoting these advantages is crucial for attracting and retaining dedicated volunteers, which improves the sustainability of mentoring as a protective factor.

Mentors cultivate a range of valuable transferable skills, including leadership, coaching, improved communication (including active listening and providing constructive feedback), and enhanced interpersonal abilities.

The responsibility associated with guiding and supporting a mentee, and the reward of witnessing their progress, can reaffirm a mentor's own abilities and insights, leading to increased self-confidence. The process also encourages personal growth, self-reflection, and enhances self-awareness, all of which add significantly to a mentor's professional and personal skillsets.

In the period after the formal mentoring relationship, many mentors report a profound sense of personal fulfillment derived from contributing to a young person's growth and well-being. This can translate into increased job and personal satisfaction, with mentors often describing their work and relationships as more meaningful. Some research even suggests that mentors experience lower levels of anxiety compared to non-mentors.

Engaging with a young person from a potentially different background can offer mentors new perspectives on societal issues and youth culture, expanding their ability to connect with their colleagues and the wider community. Mentoring can also provide opportunities to expand professional and personal networks, and can be a source of career rejuvenation, reigniting passion and providing a sense of purpose.

These reciprocal benefits underscore that mentoring is a mutually enriching endeavor, contributing significantly to adult development and well-being. This "dual benefit" aspect is not merely a positive biproduct, but a crucial factor for the long-term sustainability and scalability of mentoring programs. Programs that successfully attract and retain mentors often do so because the experience is genuinely rewarding and developmental for the adults involved. A motivated and engaged mentor pool, sustained by these intrinsic and extrinsic rewards, is essential for reaching the number of youths in need.

As we have seen, the skills that mentors develop are not confined to the mentoring relationship. These are highly valuable attributes that mentors carry back into their professional roles, family lives, and other community engagements. Consequently, a community that actively fosters mentoring is also investing in its own human capital, cultivating individuals with stronger interpersonal and leadership capabilities. In this sense, supporting mentoring programs yields a broader societal return by enhancing the overall skill set and empathetic capacity of the community.

Expanding Networks for Mentees and Mentors

Mentoring relationships serve as powerful conduits for building social capital, which refers to the networks of relationships among people who live and work in a particular society, enabling that society to function effectively. For mentees, particularly those from disadvantaged backgrounds or with limited familial support, mentors can open doors to new connections, information, and opportunities that might otherwise be inaccessible. A mentor can introduce a young person to professionals in a field of interest, provide guidance for navigating their educational or career pathways, and serve as an advocate on their behalf. This expansion of their social network can be invaluable for future success.

Mentors, too, can benefit from an expansion of their networks and exposure to different perspectives through their engagement with mentees and the broader mentoring program community. They may connect with other mentors, program staff, and community stakeholders, enriching their own social and professional lives.

For many young individuals, especially those from marginalized communities or lacking parental support systems, access to influential networks and the implicit knowledge that facilitates educational, and career progression is often limited. Social capital is a critical resource, and mentoring can act as a powerful equalizer.

By connecting youth with adults from different socio-economic or professional spheres, mentoring programs provide a vital conduit to otherwise unavailable or unimaginable networks and opportunities. This deliberate cultivation of social capital can help to mitigate systemic inequalities, offering disadvantaged youth a more level playing field and tangibly improving their life trajectories. Improving the outlook for young people can have dramatic positive impacts on their ability to withstand violent extremism and radicalization

Chapter 30: Mentoring Offers Alternatives

Mentorship offers a nuanced and individualized approach to preventing radicalization by addressing core vulnerabilities that extremist groups often exploit, fostering critical thinking skills, and providing positive life pathways.

Belonging, Identity, and Purpose

Extremist groups are effective at exploiting vulnerabilities in youth, such as social isolation, economic hardship, perceived personal grievances, and a search for deeper meaning by offering a seductive, albeit false, sense of belonging, identity, and purpose by taking advantage of developmental phases that can interrupt critical thinking. The mentor-mentee relationship can directly counteract these "pull factors." A strong, positive relationship provides a genuine source of connection, validation, and support, fulfilling the fundamental human need for belonging in a healthy, constructive way. This can diminish the appeal of extremist groups that promise camaraderie but often deliver manipulation and harm.

Adolescents can often feel personally insignificant and may be desperate to feel a sense of purpose or belonging, or to solidify a sense of identity. These factors are often identified as key psychological drivers of young people toward violence or radicalization. Mentoring can play a crucial role in helping young people develop a positive and resilient sense of self and find significance through prosocial achievements and contributions. By affirming a mentee's worth, giving them opportunities to explore their talents, and helping them set and achieve meaningful goals, mentors guide them towards constructing a positive identity, making them less susceptible to extremist narratives that offer simplistic and destructive alternative identities. Canada's national strategy on countering radicalization to violence identifies a "sense of belonging" as a common reason individuals join extremist groups, and concurrently lists "positive influences of credible friends, family members or mentors" as a key protective factor. Mentors, by their very function, provide an alternative, positive source of belonging and guidance.

Fostering Critical Thinking and Media Literacy

In an era where extremist narratives are readily accessible online, often packaged in sophisticated and manipulative ways, the ability to think critically and evaluate information is paramount. Mentors are uniquely positioned to foster these skills in young people. They can facilitate discussions that encourage questioning, analysis of sources, and recognition of propaganda techniques, thereby arming them with the tools and critical thinking skills that allow all of us to recognize extremist propaganda.

Mentors can guide youth in developing literacy across all the disparate channels of information, including digital media and news sources, helping them understand how online algorithms can create echo chambers that reinforce biased views and how extremist groups exploit digital environments. By encouraging healthy, informed skepticism towards online information and discussing diverse perspectives, mentors empower youth to navigate the complex information landscape more safely and to resist ideological conditioning.

Transforming Destructive Trajectories

A mentor helps a mentee locate or establish a pathway into the future, illustrating the different routes and outcomes that certain paths make more likely. That path offers a powerful framework for understanding how mentoring can steer individuals away from violent extremism. Building that pathway involves supporting the mentee in managing education, work, personal challenges, and life in general, with the goal of allowing the mentee to choose the path that offers the most desired and affirming destination.

This process is characterized by two essential qualities: safety and challenge. The mentor must first create a safe, trusting environment where the mentee feels secure enough to discuss sensitive or even dangerous topics. Simultaneously, the mentoring process must involve a constructive challenge to the mentee's potentially destructive perspectives, guiding them towards more positive and societally grounded ways of engaging with the world and addressing grievances.

This approach involves developing general life skills related to relationships, daily structure, community participation, emotional awareness, pragmatic and ethical decision-making, empathy, and navigating societal perspectives. By strengthening these capacities, mentoring helps young people build a stable and meaningful life, reducing the appeal of extremist ideologies that depend on chaos, hopelessness, or a distorted sense of justice as recruiting tools.

Offering Alternative Narratives and Positive Pathways

Mentors can play a vital role in exposing youth to a wider range of perspectives, opportunities, and positive life narratives that directly counter the narrow and often hateful ideologies peddled by extremist groups. They can introduce mentees to success stories, diverse career paths, avenues for civic engagement, and constructive ways to address grievances. This broadening of horizons is crucial, as many Preventing and Countering Violent Extremism (P/CVE) programs have been critiqued for simplistic understandings of youth motivations.

Engaging youth as partners in co-creating narratives of hope and positive futures, a role mentors can facilitate, is a more empowering approach. Evidence from tertiary prevention programs (focused on individuals already involved in extremism) indicates that components like education, vocational training, and socialization are more successful than direct ideological confrontation. This suggests that preventative mentoring should similarly emphasize building these positive life pathways, offering tangible alternatives to extremism.

The journey towards radicalization is often highly personal and varied. Generic, broad-based prevention programs may fail to address the specific constellation of needs, grievances, and vulnerabilities that make a particular young person more or less susceptible. Mentoring, by its very nature, offers a tailored, individualized intervention. A mentor can understand the unique circumstances of their mentee, listen to their specific concerns, and adapt their support accordingly. This personalized approach, often cited as a strength in programs for those already engaged in extremism, is equally, if not more, critical at the preventative stage. It allows for a nuanced response that can address the root causes of vulnerability far more effectively than one-size-fits-all initiatives.

Moreover, effective mentoring in the context of radicalization prevention often requires a delicate balance. It necessitates providing a safe, non-judgmental, and trusting space where a young person feels comfortable sharing potentially sensitive or problematic thoughts and associations. However, the aim is transformation and a shift in perspective. This means that mentors must also be equipped to constructively challenge harmful beliefs or ideologies and guide the mentee towards legal, non-violent, and prosocial alternatives. This dialectic of "safety and challenge" is more complex than general supportive mentoring and underscores the potential need for specialized training for mentors working with youth identified as being at higher risk of radicalization. Such training would equip them with the skills to navigate these difficult conversations effectively and ethically.

A proactive stance is also more beneficial than a purely reactive one. Rather than waiting to counter extremist ideologies after a young person has already encountered and perhaps begun to internalize them, mentoring can work proactively. By building general resilience, fostering critical thinking skills, and promoting media literacy *before* significant exposure to extremist narratives, mentoring can act as a form of psychological inoculation. If these foundational skills are developed early, youth are better equipped to recognize, question, and resist manipulative propaganda from the outset. This suggests that universal or widely available mentoring programs that incorporate these elements could serve as a broad-based preventative measure, strengthening a larger cohort of young people against the allure of radicalizing influences.

Chapter 31: Isolation and a Mental Health Crises

The COVID-19 pandemic left an indelible mark on the mental health and social well-being of young people, creating a new urgency for supportive interventions like mentoring.

Amplified Challenges for Youth

The public health measures enacted during the COVID-19 pandemic, particularly social distancing and school closures, led to unprecedented levels of social isolation for many young people. This isolation contributed significantly to a range of negative mental health outcomes, including self-esteem, depression, abuse by caregivers, and increased rates of suicide.

Mentors working with youth during this period frequently reported concerns about their mentees' overall mental health, feelings of isolation, and struggles with academic engagement. Youth served by therapeutic mentoring programs, often already contending with adverse experiences or at-risk backgrounds, likely found these existing vulnerabilities exacerbated by the pandemic's pervasive stressors. This amplified distress and disconnection can increase susceptibility to various negative influences, including the grooming tactics of extremist groups, which often target individuals who feel isolated, misunderstood, or are actively seeking connection online.

Combating Loneliness and Rebuilding Connection

In the face of such widespread challenges, mentoring relationships often served as a crucial lifeline, providing essential social and emotional support. Mentors and mentoring programs faced a sudden and dramatic shift to virtual relationships, and mentees without reliable access to home internet were often no longer able to access their scholastic or mentoring supports. Research shows that the consistent presence of an adult can reduce feelings of social isolation and loneliness. Additional findings indicate that interventions, including mentoring, can alleviate loneliness by improving social skills, enhancing social support networks, or helping to alter maladaptive cognitions related to social connection.

Indeed, mentors are immensely powerful vehicles for addressing loneliness and social isolation in youth, and community-based mentoring has been identified as one potential solution to this pervasive issue. The consistent, caring presence of a mentor can act as a powerful antidote to loneliness, helping young people to feel seen, heard, and valued, and facilitating their re-engagement with social activities and peer relationships as pandemic restrictions eased.

Adapting to the New Normal

The pandemic necessitated a rapid shift in how mentoring services were delivered, largely toward online platforms. E-mentoring, utilizing text, video chat, and other digital tools, became (and remains) a common mode of connection. While this transition presented challenges, such as unequal access to technology and concerns about privacy in shared living spaces, it also showed the potential of e-mentoring to reach youth, especially those in remote areas or facing mobility restrictions. Research suggests that e-mentoring, though a relatively new field, does show promise, and tailored technology-based interventions, can be effective.

The benefits of e-mentoring include increased accessibility and the ability to maintain continuity of support during disruptions. However, the challenges, including the digital divide, the potential for lower-quality interpersonal connection compared to in-person interactions, and the need for specific training for mentors in digital engagement, must be carefully considered and addressed as e-mentoring continues to evolve as part of the "new normal."

The rise of e-mentoring, while offering undeniable benefits in terms of reach and continuity, particularly during periods of enforced isolation, also presents a complex dynamic. Increased reliance on online platforms for positive engagement, such as mentoring, may inadvertently increase overall screen time for young people. This heightened online presence, if not carefully navigated, could also increase exposure to online risks, including the very extremist propaganda and recruitment efforts that mentoring seeks to counteract. Therefore, while e-mentoring is a valuable tool, its implementation must be thoughtfully coupled with digital literacy training for both mentors and mentees. Mentors, in an e-mentoring context, take on an even more critical role in guiding young people's online navigation, helping them to discern credible information from misinformation and to recognize and report harmful content. Strategies must ensure that the digital tools intended for support do not unintentionally amplify vulnerability to negative online influences.

A Specialized Approach for Heightened Needs

For young people experiencing more significant mental health challenges, potentially intensified by the pandemic, a more specialized approach known as therapeutic mentoring may be beneficial. Therapeutic mentoring aims explicitly to "reduce negative mental health symptoms and increase psychological well-being". It is often delivered by paraprofessionals, such as trained volunteers or students, under the supervision of licensed mental health practitioners, and incorporates evidence-based practices. Youth referred to such programs have often faced substantial adverse experiences or are considered at high risk.

While the field calls for more rigorous research to clearly define its parameters and establish its efficacy through randomized controlled trials, the urgent need to expand the mental health workforce with well-trained paraprofessionals, including mentors, is widely acknowledged, especially given the increased demand for mental health support post-pandemic. Therapeutic mentoring, often serving as an additive to other forms of mental health care, represents an intensive form of support that could be particularly relevant for addressing the deeper-seated mental health issues that have emerged or worsened in the wake of COVID-19.

The widespread mental health impact of the pandemic suggests a broader need for what might be termed *therapeutic-lite* mentoring. While formal therapeutic mentoring is designed for youth with clearly defined and often more severe needs, involving specifically trained paraprofessionals, a much larger cohort of young people now experience sub-clinical mental health struggles, such as heightened anxiety or persistent low mood, because of pandemic-related stressors. This implies that all mentors, even those in general community or school-based programs, would benefit significantly from enhanced training in mental health literacy.

Such training should include understanding common mental health challenges in youth, principles of trauma-informed care, recognizing warning signs that indicate a need for more specialized help, and knowing appropriate referral pathways. Equipping mentors with these skills does not attempt to turn them into therapists but enables them to create a more understanding, supportive, and responsive mentoring environment, enhancing the therapeutic potential of all mentoring relationships.

The disruptions caused by the pandemic to education, social development, and routine activities have created a imperative for mentoring programs to help students catch up to previously established benchmarks. Beyond simply maintaining well-being or preventing future problems, mentoring in the post-pandemic landscape must actively help youth recover lost ground. This includes addressing learning gaps through academic support, facilitating the redevelopment of social-emotional skills that may have stagnated or regressed during periods of isolation, and encouraging re-engagement with community activities.

For some students, mentors provided crucial academic and emotional support during the pandemic. Moving forward, programs should be intentionally designed to support this multifaceted recovery process, positioning mentoring as a key mechanism for helping young people not only to cope but also to rebuild and thrive.

Chapter 32: Effective Mentoring Programs

The success of mentoring as an intervention depends on the program design, mentor training, quantity and quality of recruited mentors, and the implementation and tracking of program elements. Adherence to evidence-based practices across the lifecycle of the mentoring relationship is crucial for achieving positive outcomes for youth and building improvements into future iterations.

Hallmarks of Successful Mentoring Programs

Effective mentoring programs are built on a foundation of clear purpose, strong organizational practices, and a commitment to quality. Programs should have a well-defined mission statement, specifically measured objectives, and a logical model or theory of change that outlines how their activities are expected to lead to desired and predictable outcomes.

Program design and operations should be informed by research on effective mentoring, such as MENTOR's *Elements of Effective Practice for Mentoring*.

Careful consideration of costs, potential legal liabilities, organizational structure, and organizational capacity to evaluate and continuously monitor improvement are crucial elements, requiring strong program management and organizational leadership. Staff should possess a solid understanding of youth mentoring research and best practices, with opportunities for continued learning.

Building support within the school or broader community is vital. For student-led initiatives, the active engagement of school leaders in addressing systemic challenges and investing in universal prevention is crucial for success. While structure is important, programs should also allow for flexibility to meet individual mentee needs and foster natural relationship development.

The effectiveness of mentoring can vary significantly depending on program characteristics and the quality of implementation. Continuous monitoring and improvement are therefore essential. It is also vital that mentoring organizations remain mindful of their capacity to support the mentee population to not degrade mentor quality to serve the largest possible group. The scale of any program must be effectively managed.

Recruitment, Screening, Training, and Support

Ensuring a pool of high-quality, well-supported mentors is paramount for program success and, most importantly, for the safety and well-being of mentees. This involves careful attention to each stage of the mentor-mentee relationship lifecycle.

Programs need strategic approaches to recruit a diverse and committed group of mentors. Rigorous screening processes, including criminal and civil background checks and interviews, are essential to ensure that mentors are suitable and safe to work with young people. *This is a non-negotiable aspect of responsible program management.*

Comprehensive initial and ongoing training for mentors is a critical component of effective programs. Research shows that Enhanced Mentoring, which includes pre- and post-match mentor training, is associated with better outcomes for all participants.

Training should cover topics such as youth development stages and needs, effective communication and active listening skills, building trust and rapport, setting appropriate boundaries, and understanding cultural humility and implementing culturally responsive practices.

It is also crucial to integrate the principles and practices of trauma-informed care into any youth-serving program. Recognizing signs of distress, including mental health challenges and potential indicators of radicalization should bolster every interaction with a student or other youth.

Mentors also require continuous support to navigate challenges, prevent burnout, and enhance their skills. This includes regular check-ins with program staff, opportunities for peer support among mentors, and access to additional training or resources as needed. While a single mentor may have multiple simultaneous mentees, monitoring should include steps to prevent the mentor from becoming over-committed, unintentionally reducing the mentor's quality through a desire to help as many young people as possible. Monitoring the progress of matches helps ensure relationship quality and allows for timely intervention if problems arise.

The Art and Science of Matching

Creating successful mentor-mentee pairings is both an art and a science. While there is no single formula, thoughtful matching can significantly enhance the likelihood of a positive and enduring relationship.

Mentor matching is recognized as a core standard of effective mentoring practice. Programs often aim to pair mentors and mentees based on shared interests, values, or personality traits, as this can provide an initial foundation for connection. However, deeper compatibility factors, such as the mentee's specific developmental needs, the mentor's strengths and experience, and mutual expectations for the relationship, are also crucial.

While some research suggests that a mentor's race or socio-economic status may not be the primary determinant of outcomes compared to factors like interaction frequency and relationship quality, it is also noted that mentoring can have greater impacts for youth of color. This underscores the importance of culturally sensitive matching processes and ensuring that mentors are trained in cultural humility to effectively connect with youth from diverse backgrounds.

Recognizing the importance of representation in role-modeling and leadership, it is important that community members of color be given every opportunity to act as mentors to as many young people as possible.

Where feasible and appropriate, involving both potential mentors and mentees (and their families) in the matching process can increase buy-in and satisfaction. Ultimately, the goal is to create a match where a genuine, trusting, and emotionally bonded relationship can flourish, as these relational qualities are strongly associated with better outcomes for youth.

Peer-to-Peer or Adult-Child Models

Both peer-to-peer and adult-child mentoring models offer distinct advantages and can be applied effectively depending on program goals and the target population.

Adult-child mentoring is the most common model and has a substantial evidence base supporting its effectiveness. Programs like Big Brothers Big Sisters have demonstrated significant positive impacts on reducing delinquency, substance use, and aggression, while improving academic and social outcomes. Adult mentors can offer valuable life experience, broader perspectives, access to wider networks, and a different form of guidance and authority that can be beneficial for navigating complex life decisions that adolescents are developmentally unable to manage without guidance.

Peer-to-peer mentoring changes the relationship dynamic by leveraging the relatability and shared experiences of individuals who are closer in age. Student-led clubs focusing on violence or substance use prevention often utilize peer mentoring approaches. Research on programs like "Saving Lives, Inspiring Youth" indicates that serving as a peer mentor can also yield benefits for the mentors themselves, including reduced aggression. While the evaluation research for cross-age peer mentoring is less extensive than for adult-child models, it is widely recognized as an effective strategy. Peer mentors may be particularly effective in fostering social integration, addressing peer-specific challenges (like bullying or social dynamics), and modeling positive behaviors in a way that feels relevant to younger mentees.

The choice of model may depend on specific program objectives. For instance, if the goal is broad life guidance and access to professional networks, adult mentoring might be preferred. If the aim is to improve school climate, reduce bullying, or enhance social skills among peers, a peer mentoring program may be highly effective. In some cases, a combination of approaches or opportunities for both types of mentoring could be beneficial. In either case, programming oversight by appropriately trained staff is important.

Ensuring Positive Transitions

Structured, program-initiated mentoring relationships are not intended to last forever; most are set according to a school calendar or annual basis. Knowing that the relationship will eventually end (or change, as many mentor-mentee matches remain in contact for years afterward), make it important to acknowledge and prepare for the end early and regularly throughout the period. The conclusion of a formal mentoring relationship is a critical stage that may be overlooked but has significant implications for the well-being of both mentor and mentee.

Planned and thoughtful closure is a core standard of effective mentoring practice; abrupt or poorly managed endings can leave mentees, particularly vulnerable and at-risk youth, feeling abandoned or confused, potentially undermining the gains realized during the relationship. This is especially important for youth in foster care, who the research tells us are more likely to experience sudden disruption or premature closure of mentoring relationships.

Effective closure involves advanced planning, discussing the end of the formal relationship in advance, and as early as possible. Providing opportunities for both mentor and mentee to reflect on their experiences, achievements, and what they have learned from each other is another core element of this process. Acknowledging feelings, validating any emotions associated with the ending of the relationship is crucial in preventing resentment feelings of disregard, and in sustaining a lasting sense of regard in the mentee.

Some mentors may want to discuss expectations and possibilities for any future, less formal contact, if appropriate and in line with program guidelines. Helping the mentee identify other sources of support and connect with future opportunities is also a valuable service that can be offered by the mentor. A well-managed closure process helps to solidify the gains made during the mentoring relationship and allows both individuals to move forward positively.

The successful implementation of mentoring programs, particularly those aiming to address complex issues like radicalization prevention and significant post-pandemic mental health needs, demands more than generic approaches.

While foundational mentor training in youth development and communication is essential, the specific nature of these challenges necessitates specialized training. Mentors need to be equipped to recognize early warning signs of radicalization, understand the attraction to extremist narratives and grooming tactics, be proficient in trauma-informed care principles, and know the appropriate and safe referral pathways when a mentee's needs exceed their capacity or the program's scope. Without such specialized preparation, mentors may inadvertently miss critical signals or respond in ways that are ineffective or even counterproductive.

The impact of mentoring programs can be significantly amplified through thoughtful partnerships between schools and community organizations. Schools provide unparalleled access to large populations of youth and possess existing infrastructure and staff already trained to identify students who might benefit from mentoring. Community organizations, on the other hand, often bring specialized expertise in youth development, mental health services, or specific intervention models, and can offer support that extends beyond school hours and into the broader community. The success of student-led peer mentoring initiatives, for example, is often contingent on school leaders actively addressing systemic challenges and fostering a supportive environment. A collaborative model, where schools play a role in identification and referral, and community organizations contribute trained mentors and specialized programming, creates a more comprehensive, accessible, and sustainable ecosystem for supporting young people.

The ultimate effectiveness of mentoring is determined not merely by the presence of a mentor, but by an interplay of dosage and quality. "Dosage," in this sense, refers to quantifiable aspects of mentoring relationships, including the frequency and duration of each interaction, and the overall length of the mentoring relationship. "Quality" here refers to the experiential aspects, including the level of trust and emotional bond established, the relevance and engagement of activities, and the mentor's personal ability to provide empathetic support and constructive guidance.

Evidence, perhaps unsurprisingly, indicates that longer, more frequent interactions between a mentor and mentee, and the associated increased levels of trust and emotional bond with a mentor, are directly tied to stronger school performance and positive behavioral changes. Program design must therefore be intentional in fostering both sufficient quantity and quality of every interaction. This may involve setting clear expectations for both parties regarding contact time, providing resources and suggestions for engaging activities, and offering ongoing support and coaching to mentors to help them build and maintain strong, impactful relationships.

Chapter 33: Sustaining Mentoring Initiatives

To fully realize the protective power of mentoring, concerted efforts are needed at policy, systemic, and programmatic levels to sustain, scale, and continuously improve mentoring initiatives.

Greater recognition and support for mentoring from policymakers are essential for its widespread implementation and sustainability. Program leaders and advocates should be advocate for community awareness of youth mentoring and (politely) demand adequate resources from public and private sources.

It is important to advocate for stable and dedicated funding streams at local, state, and national levels to support the operational costs of mentoring programs, including staff salaries, mentor training, and program resources. Public and private initiatives, such as Canada's Community Resilience Fund (www.publicsafety.gc.ca), which supports research and programs to counter radicalization, and Connecticut's Governor's Prevention Partnership (www.gppct.org), which employs mentoring as a strategy to prevent youth substance use, can serve as models in these efforts.

Programs at every level should promote policies that facilitate partnerships between schools, community organizations, businesses, and government agencies to create a more integrated mentoring ecosystem. Encouraging policies that allow or incentivize employees to volunteer as mentors during work hours, expanding the pool of available mentors, are also effective.

We will be able to widely recognize mentoring as a key prevention strategy through advocacy for the formal inclusion of mentoring in broader public health, education, and safety strategies aimed at youth violence prevention, mental health promotion, and countering violent extremism.

Schools, Mental Health, and Juvenile Justice

Mentoring should not be viewed as a standalone, isolated intervention but rather as a strategic component of a comprehensive continuum of support services for youth. Its effectiveness can be significantly enhanced when integrated into existing systems.

School-based mentoring programs, including peer mentoring initiatives, can be embedded within school safety plans and student support services. Schools, when properly staffed and trained, play a key role in identifying students who would benefit from mentoring, and in building connections with community-based programs.

Given the urgent need to expand the behavioral health workforce, well-trained mentors and therapeutic mentoring programs can serve as valuable paraprofessionals, often working as an adjunct to formal mental health care. A mentor can also act as a supplementary referral pathway for youth experiencing mild to moderate mental health challenges or those needing support in conjunction with clinical treatment.

Mentoring has shown immense promise for young people already involved in, or at risk of involvement with, the juvenile justice system. Advocacy-based mentoring and group mentoring models have been linked to reduced re-arrests and misconduct, and youth with mentors are less likely to become involved with the behaviors and actions that often lead to law enforcement intervention. Integrating mentoring into diversion programs, probation services, and re-entry initiatives can provide crucial support for positive reintegration and reduced recidivism. Youth who become involved in the justice system are more than 80 percent more likely than their peers to become incarcerated as adults, so preventing that initial interaction has a lifelong impact.

This systemic integration ensures that mentoring is more accessible, reaches more youth through multiple touchpoints, and complements other forms of support, creating a more holistic and effective safety net.

Chapter 34: Mentoring a More Resilient Generation

The convergence of persistent youth violence, the evolving threat of radicalization, and the profound mental health and social consequence of the COVID-19 pandemic has created an urgent need for effective, evidence-based interventions. Mentorship, in both peer-to-peer and adult-child configurations, stands out as a powerful protective factor and a catalyst for positive development.

The Critical Role of Mentoring

Mentoring relationships offer a unique and deeply personal form of support that can buffer young people against a wide array of risks. By providing consistent emotional support, positive role modeling, and guidance in developing essential life skills, mentors help to build self-esteem, enhance social-emotional competencies, improve academic engagement, and reduce negative behaviors, including aggression and substance use. These same mechanisms make mentoring a vital tool in preventing radicalization towards violence. Mentors can counteract the lure of extremist groups by fostering a genuine sense of belonging and purpose, equipping youth with critical thinking skills that enable them to resist manipulative narratives and help them establish a positive view of the future through constructive pathways.

In the post-COVID-19 landscape of amplified youth isolation and mental health crises, the role of mentoring has become even more essential. Mentors have served as lifelines, combating loneliness, facilitating re-connection, and supporting young people through unprecedented challenges, with programs adapting to embrace e-mentoring. The development of personal and professional skills is not limited to mentees; mentors also experience significant growth, enhancing the sustainability and appeal of these initiatives.

The expenditure on well-designed and implemented mentoring programs should not be viewed as a cost but as a strategic investment in human capital, community safety, and future societal well-being. Evidence strongly suggests that mentoring can reduce absenteeism, delinquency, substance abuse, and violence, while improving academic achievement and mental health outcomes. These positive outcomes translate into significant long-term benefits for our wider society, including reduced healthcare costs, diminished reliance on the criminal justice system, and increased economic productivity from a more skilled and stable workforce. Funding and championing mentoring initiatives is a cost-effective strategy that prevents more expensive social problems from taking root and helps to build a stronger, more resilient, and more productive generation of future leaders.

The evidence supporting the benefits of mentoring, in my view, should serve as a collective call to action directed at educators, policymakers, community leaders, researchers, and all individuals who are in the privileged position to support young people.

Educators and school administrators are able to champion the integration of mentoring programs within school systems. They can foster school environments that support peer mentoring initiatives and collaborate with community-based organizations to connect students with adult mentors, but only when they are, in turn, supported by their districts.

Policymakers can prioritize mentoring in public funding and policy agendas, developing and supporting policies that provide sustainable funding for evidence-based mentoring programs, encourage cross-sector partnerships, and promote quality standards. It is imperative that we convince elected officials to recognize mentoring as a key preventative strategy in education, public health, and community safety initiatives.

Building and expanding access to high-quality mentoring programs is work that is best undertaken by community leaders – non-profit organizations, business owners, faith-based organizations, and others in a position to interact with large sections of the population. These individuals can work to recruit diverse mentors, provide them with excellent training and support, and ensure that programs are responsive to the specific needs of the youth in their communities, all while fostering collaboration in the creation of a sustainable network of support.

No matter who we are as individuals, we should all consider becoming mentors. The commitment of time and empathy can profoundly alter the trajectory of a young person's life, offering them guidance, support, and a belief in their potential.

It is also important to recognize that effective mentoring empowers youth to become agents of positive change themselves. By fostering skills, confidence, and a sense of purpose, mentoring equips young people not only to navigate their own challenges but also to contribute positively to their communities.

Postscript

Our journey together through these pages has explored the multifaceted dimensions of school safety, uncovering the profound challenges and transformative opportunities that define this critical issue. From understanding the root causes of school violence, to advocating for comprehensive, proactive strategies, the path forward is (hopefully) clear but undoubtedly intimidating. I hope that it has become evident that achieving sustainable, meaningful change requires collective action, unwavering commitment, and a shared vision for a better future.

At the foundation of my vision for holistic school safety and positive school safety climates is the recognition that school safety is not merely about responding to catastrophic events, such as shootings or other acts of extreme violence. It must begin with the daily experiences of students and staff, addressing issues like bullying, psychological well-being, and the broader social factors that influence behavior. The interconnectedness of violence within schools, homes, and communities cannot be dismissed, and a systemic approach that considers the broader context of students' lives must be adopted.

In the chapters dedicated to cultivating positive school climates and integrating Social and Emotional Learning (SEL), I tried to emphasize the importance of creating environments where students feel valued, supported, and connected. SEL equips students with the skills to navigate challenges, build relationships, and make responsible decisions. Similarly, restorative justice practices focus on repairing harm and fostering a sense of community, moving beyond punitive responses to conflicts and promoting a culture of empathy and accountability.

Proactive measures like comprehensive mental health systems and restorative justice practices are critical. These strategies address the underlying causes of student behavior and provide students with the support they need to thrive. The evidence is clear: schools that prioritize mental health, equity, and restorative approaches experience fewer incidents of violence and improved overall well-being for their students and staff than those that rely solely on punitive and reactive measures.

Sustainable change requires systemic reform, supported by ongoing advocacy and intentional policy initiatives. The chapters on building community support, crafting behavioral health-centered policies, and securing sustainable financial strategies showed the necessity of aligning resources and priorities at every level—from local communities to state and federal governments.

Holistic safety, as outlined here, requires investing in protective factors beyond bulletproof windows and armed security; it requires a person-first approach. The power of mentoring can be harnessed in this way, taking advantage of its transformative potential in preventing violence and fostering resilience. Effective mentoring programs address isolation, build critical social connections, and provide students with role models who guide them toward positive paths. This protective factor can fundamentally alter the trajectory of a student's life, breaking cycles of violence and promoting personal growth.

I want to close by emphasizing the responsibility of every individual to act. Schools are not just institutions for learning; they are communities where young minds and hearts are shaped. To truly lift the lockdown – both metaphorically and literally – requires a shift in mindset, policy, and practice. Each of us may not be able to dedicate the time or energy to mentoring, but we can write letters to our representatives or speak at local government meetings.

We must foster environments where every student feels safe, seen, and supported, and invest in professional development to implement SEL and restorative practices effectively. We must come to understand the impact of trauma on students' behavior and learning and adopt trauma-informed practices to best care for each student. And we must work together to build systems that offer support and healing rather than punishment.

This book is not intended to end the discussion, nor do I believe that the information or opinions shared here are all-inclusive. It is incumbent upon each of us to continue engaging with these important topics. We're all responsible for staying informed about evidence-based strategies and innovative practices in school safety.

We all have the potential to collaborate with educators to create a unified front for student well-being, and to advocate for policies that prioritize safety and mental health. When we model the behaviors we hope to see in others, we become participants in our children's lives, providing guidance, support, and a safe space for open communication. In an age where cyberbullying and online harassment are pervasive, teach children to navigate the digital world responsibly and respectfully.

My message to policymakers is simple: advocate for laws that address the full spectrum of safety needs, from mental health funding to restorative justice frameworks, don't just settle for the appearance of safety by turning schools into prisons. Ensure that schools have the resources to implement comprehensive safety strategies without compromising other educational priorities.

While the challenges are significant, the potential for positive change is greater still. Every small action, every conversation, and every effort to prioritize safety and well-being contributes to a larger movement that can transform our schools and communities. The strategies outlined in this book are not mere aspirations; they are actionable steps grounded in evidence and experience.

As we move forward, consider how we can be catalysts for change. Whether through mentoring, advocacy, or simply by being an active participant in our local communities. Together, we can create a future where schools are not just places of learning, but are community hubs for growth, connection, and hope.

I can imagine a world where every student walks into school without fear, where they are met with compassion and support, and where their potential is nurtured in an environment that celebrates diversity, resilience, and collaboration. This is the future I hope we can strive for, a future where holistic safety is not an ideal but a reality.

I am committed to lifting the lockdown by breaking free from outdated mindsets and practices that limit our progress. The path is clear, the tools are available, and the time to act is now. Together, we can build a safer, more supportive world for our children and for generations to come.

Appendices

Appendix A: Glossary of Terms

Availability Bias: Also called the availability *heuristic*. A cognitive bias where people tend to overestimate the likelihood of events if they can be easily recalled or imagined. This bias occurs because information that is more readily available in our minds is perceived as being more frequent or probable than information that is more difficult to retrieve.

Braided Funding: A strategy that involves coordinating multiple funding sources (federal, state, local, private) to support a unified program or set of services, while keeping the accounting for each funding stream separate to meet individual reporting requirements.

Community Schools: Schools that partner with families and community organizations to integrate academics, health and social services, youth and community development, and community engagement to improve student learning, strengthen families, and build healthier communities.

Crisis Prevention and Intervention: Strategies and protocols developed to address the multifaceted nature of potential crises and prioritize the behavioral health and well-being of students and staff.

Cyberbullying: A pervasive issue involving repeated aggressive behavior intended to harm or intimidate, extended to a digital platform made possible by the rise of social media and online communication.

Exclusionary Discipline: Disciplinary practices, such as suspensions and expulsions, that remove students from the learning environment.

Hate Crimes: Offenses motivated by an implicit or explicit bias against a victim's perceived race, religion, sexual orientation, or other protected class of characteristics.

Holistic School Safety: A comprehensive, multi-layered, and proactive approach to creating safe and supportive learning environments that addresses the physical, emotional, and psychological well-being of all students and staff. It emphasizes positive school climate, mental health support, restorative practices, staff and student engagement, and family/community partnerships over sole reliance on physical security measures.

Immediate Action Rapid Deployment (IARD): A protocol that trains first responding officers, even a single officer, to move directly toward the sound of gunfire to neutralize a shooter and stop the killing.

Multi-Tiered System of Supports (MTSS): A framework that schools use to provide a continuum of academic, behavioral, and social-emotional support to students based on their needs. Tier 1 provides universal support for all students, Tier 2 offers targeted interventions for some students, and Tier 3 delivers intensive, individualized support for a few students.

Positive Behavioral Interventions and Supports (PBIS): A proactive, evidence-based framework for improving school climate and student behavior outcomes by teaching and reinforcing positive behavior expectations.

Radicalization: A process whereby individuals adopt ideologies that justify the use of violence to achieve specific goals.

Restorative Justice / Restorative Practices (RJ/RP): A philosophy and set of practices focused on repairing harm and building relationships when wrongdoing occurs, rather than solely on punishment. It emphasizes accountability, empathy, and the involvement of all affected parties in finding solutions.

School Climate: The quality and character of school life, reflecting norms, goals, values, interpersonal relationships, teaching and learning practices, and organizational structures. It includes dimensions such as safety, engagement, support, and environment.

School Resource Officer (SRO): A sworn law enforcement officer assigned to work in schools. In holistic models, their role is ideally focused on safety planning, emergency preparedness, education, and mentoring, rather than routine discipline.

School-to-Prison Pipeline: The process by which students, particularly those from disadvantaged backgrounds and minority groups, become involved with the juvenile and criminal justice systems due to non-criminal behavior.

Social-Emotional Learning (SEL): The process through which individuals acquire and apply the knowledge, skills, and attitudes to develop healthy identities, manage emotions, achieve goals, feel and show empathy, establish supportive relationships, and make responsible decisions. Core competencies often include self-awareness, self-management, social awareness, relationship skills, and responsible decision-making.

Specialized Instructional Support Personnel (SISP): A collective term often used for school counselors, psychologists, and social workers.

Therapeutic Mentoring: A specialized approach to mentoring that explicitly aims to reduce negative mental health symptoms and increase psychological well-being, often delivered by paraprofessionals under supervision of licensed mental health practitioners.

Threat Assessment Teams: Teams composed of school administrators, counselors, psychologists, and potentially law enforcement personnel who responsible for evaluating and responding to potential threats of violence made by students.

Trauma-Informed Care/Practices: An approach in human service delivery, including education, that assumes an individual is more likely than not to have a history of trauma. It recognizes the presence of trauma symptoms and acknowledges the role trauma may play in an individual's life, aiming to create environments of healing and recovery rather than practices and services that may inadvertently re-traumatize.

Zero Tolerance Policies: School or district policies that mandate predetermined, typically severe, consequences (such as suspension or expulsion) for specific student offenses, regardless of the circumstances or severity of the behavior.

Appendix B: Directory of Resources

- CASEL (Collaborative for Academic, Social, and Emotional Learning): A leading organization advancing the development of academic, social, and emotional competence for all students. Provides research, resources, and guidance on SEL. (www.casel.org)
- Committee for Children: Developer of the Second Step programs and other research-based social-emotional learning, bullying prevention, and child protection resources. (www.cfchildren.org)
- Governor's Prevention Partnership: Connecticut-based public-private partnership that uses mentoring as a tool to prevent youth substance use. (www.gppct.org)
- Learning Policy Institute (LPI): Conducts and communicates independent, high-quality research to improve education policy and practice. Publishes reports on topics like whole child education and school safety. (www.learningpolicyinstitute.org)
- MENTOR: National leader in mentoring programs for youth. The *Elements of Effective Practice* are available for free. (www.mentoring.org)
- National Association of School Psychologists (NASP): Provides resources and advocacy related to school psychology, mental health,

and safe and successful schools. (www.nasponline.org)
- National Center on Safe Supportive Learning Environments (NCSSLE): Funded by the U.S. Department of Education, offers information and technical assistance to states, districts, schools, institutions of higher learning, and communities focused on improving school climate and conditions for learning. (safesupportivelearning.ed.gov)
- National PTA: The largest volunteer child advocacy association in the United States. Provides resources and advocacy tools for parents on issues including school safety. (www.pta.org)
- Ohio School Safety Center (OSSC): Assists local schools and law enforcement with preventing, preparing for, and responding to threats and acts of violence through a holistic, solutions-based method. (ohioschoolsafetycenter.ohio.gov)
- RestorativeJustice.org (International Institute for Restorative Practices - IIRP Graduate School): Provides information, training, and resources on restorative practices.
- Safe and Sound Schools: A non-profit organization founded by parents who lost children in the Sandy Hook Elementary tragedy, dedicated to empowering communities to improve school safety. (www.safeandsoundschools.org)

- SchoolSafety.gov: A federal government website providing schools and districts with actionable recommendations, resources, and tools to create safe and supportive learning environments.
- Sandy Hook Promise: A national non-profit organization led by several family members whose loved ones were killed at Sandy Hook Elementary School, focused on preventing gun violence and other forms of violence and victimization. (www.sandyhookpromise.org)

Work Cited

1. Mental Health Technology Transfer Center Network Coordinating Office. "National School Mental Health Best Practices: Implementation Guidance Modules for States, Districts, and Schools Participant Manual." National Center for School Mental Health, 2019. https://www.schoolsafety.gov/sites/default/files/2021-09/National_SMH_Best%20Practices_Participant_Manual_Final-Mar2021.pdf.
2. Achenbach, Joel. "NRA Didn't Start out a Political Organization." Daily Herald, January 12, 2013. https://www.dailyherald.com/20130112/news/nra-didnt-start-out-a-political-organization/.
3. Adams, Oscar. "Restorative Practices." Austin ISD, 2022. https://www.austinisd.org/ed-support/restorative-practices.
4. Alaniz, Kayla, Jason R. Ingram, and Matthew B. Fuller. "Teacher Climate Configurations and School Crisis Preparedness." *Journal of School Violence*, April 20, 2025, 1–16. https://doi.org/10.1080/15388220.2025.2492755.
5. American Federation of Teachers. "Safe, Orderly and Healthy Schools Resources." American Federation of Teachers, April 26, 2023. https://www.aft.org/education/publications/safe-orderly-and-healthy-schools-resources.
6. Arizona Department of Education. "Project AWARE: Advancing Wellness and Resiliency in Education," 2018. https://www.azahcccs.gov/AHCCCS/Downloads/SuicidePrevention/AWARE_Fact%20Sheet_FY19.pdf.
7. Attendance Works. "Health, Well-Being and Safety Route - Attendance Works." Attendance Works, 2019. https://www.attendanceworks.org/resources/toolkits/the-50-challenge-crafting-a-state-road-map/the-50-challenge-step-3/health-well-being-and-safety-route/.
8. Ayoub, Lama, Lina Villegas, Elise Jensen, and Andrew Martinez. "Restorative Justice in NYC High Schools: Perceived Impact and Mixed Findings from a Randomized Controlled Trial," 2022. https://www.innovatingjustice.org/wp-content/uploads/2022/03/RJ_in_Schools.pdf.
9. Bertelsen, Preben. "Mentoring in Anti-Radicalization: A Systematic Assessment, Intervention and Supervision Tool in Mentoring," 2018. https://psy.au.dk/fileadmin/Psykologi/Forskning/Preben_Bertelsen/Artikler/Mentoring_in_anti_radicalization.pdf.
10. Bhatia, Rukmani. "Guns, Lies, and Fear." Center for American Progress, April 24, 2019. https://www.americanprogress.org/article/guns-lies-fear/.
11. Big Brothers Big Sisters. "How Mentorship Builds Self-Esteem and Empathy in Young People." Big Brothers Big Sisters of Long Island, December 30, 2024. https://bbbsli.org/how-mentorship-builds-self-esteem-in-young-people/.
12. Blad, Evie. "What Makes Schools Safe? Researchers Outline These 4 Key Recommendations." Education Week, May 7, 2025. https://www.edweek.org/leadership/what-makes-schools-safe-researchers-outlinethese-4-key-recommendations/2025/05.

13. Blanton, Megan Ann. "A 21 Year Meta Analysis of the Effectiveness of Trauma-Sensitive Schools Initiatives." JagWorks@USA, 2023. https://jagworks.southalabama.edu/theses_diss/166/.
14. Brouillette-Alarie, Sebastien, Ghayda Hassan, Sarah Ousman, Elea Savard, Deniz Kilinc, Pablo Madriaza, Wynnpaul Varela, David Pickup, and Emmanuel Danis. "Systematic Review on the Outcomes of Tertiary Prevention Programs in the Field of Violent Radicalization." *Journal for Deradicalization*, no. 42 (2025). https://jd.journals.publicknowledgeproject.org/index.php/jd/article/download/1027/515
15. California Department of Education. "Comprehensive School Safety Plans - Violence Prevention (ca Dept of Education)." www.cde.ca.gov, August 19, 2022. https://www.cde.ca.gov/ls/ss/vp/cssp.asp.
16. Cambrian. "CSD Social and Emotional Learning Curriculum." Accessed May 16, 2025. https://resources.finalsite.net/images/v1695632700/cambriansdorg/fhiv7snki9doxkqbpn0p/CSDSocialandEmotionalLearningSecondStepaViolencePreventionCurriculum.pdf.
17. Campisi, Jessica. "Study: Parental Involvement Lessens Effects of Bullying on Middle Schoolers." K-12 Dive, March 28, 2019. https://www.k12dive.com/news/study-parental-involvement-lessens-effects-of-bullying-on-middle-schoolers/551447/.
18. CASEL. "Advancing Social and Emotional Learning." Casel.org, 2023. https://casel.org/.
19. ———. "District Partnerships." CASEL, February 27, 2025. https://casel.org/about-us/our-mission-work/community-network-partners/.
20. ———. "Early Learning-Grade 8 Why Choose the Second Step Program?" Accessed May 16, 2025. https://blogcontent.summit-education.com/wp-content/uploads/CBULBS.1-Additional-Supplements.pdf.
21. ———. "How Can School Districts Elevate Student Voice? Check out Three Case Studies from across the U.S. - CASEL." CASEL.org, July 22, 2024. https://casel.org/blog/how-can-school-districts-elevate-student-voice-check-out-three-case-studies-from-across-the-us/.
22. ———. "Key Insights from the Collaborating Districts Initiative," 2017. https://drc.casel.org/uploads/sites/3/2019/02/Key-Insights-from-the-Collaborating-Districts-Initiative.pdf.
23. ———. "What Does the Research Say?" CASEL. Collaborative for Academic, Social, and Emotional Learning, 2022. https://casel.org/fundamentals-of-sel/what-does-the-research-say/.
24. Centers for Disease Control. "Parent Engagement in Schools." Healthy Youth Parent Resources, November 22, 2024. https://www.cdc.gov/healthy-youth-parent-resources/parent-engagement/index.html.
25. ———. "Promoting Mental Health and Well-Being in Schools." Mental Health Action Guide, December 3, 2024. https://www.cdc.gov/mental-health-action-guide/about/index.html.
26. ———. "School Connectedness Helps Students Thrive." Reducing Health Risks Among Youth, December 6, 2024. https://www.cdc.gov/youth-behavior/school-connectedness/index.html.
27. ———. "Youth Risk Behavior Survey Data Summary & Trends Report." Youth Risk Behavior Surveillance System (YRBSS), July 1, 2024. https://www.cdc.gov/yrbs/dstr/index.html.

28. Chellappa, Srikant. "The Role of Mentoring in Employee Skill Development." Mentoring Complete, December 9, 2023. https://www.mentoringcomplete.com/how-to-drive-employee-skill-development-with-mentoring/.
29. Coleman, Arica L. "When the NRA Supported Gun Control." Time. Time, July 29, 2016. https://time.com/4431356/nra-gun-control-history/.
30. Committee for Children. "Committee for Children | Social-Emotional Learning Programs." Committee for Children. Committee for Children, 2017. https://www.cfchildren.org/.
31. ———. "Curriculum Review Rubric Contents." Accessed May 16, 2025. https://cdn.secondstep.org/static/pdf/student-assessment/second-step-curriculum-review-rubric.pdf.
32. Cornwall, Gail. "Social Emotional Learning Can Help Prevent School Violence — Here's Why." Parents, 2022. https://www.parents.com/kids/safety/school/social-emotional-learning-can-help-prevent-school-violence-heres-why/.
33. Crisis Prevention Institute. "How Trauma-Informed Schools Help Every Student Succeed." Crisis Prevention Institute (CPI), March 31, 2021. https://www.crisisprevention.com/blog/education/how-trauma-informed-schools-help-every-student-succeed/.
34. Crocker, John, Robert Franks, Derek Sosnowski, Matthew Ma, Pecoraro, Samantha Matlin, Christopher Bellonci, Sharon Hoover, and Nancy Lever. "Mental Health and Schools: Best Practices to Support Our Students Implications for Policy, Systems, and Practice." The Baker Center, 2023. https://www.bakercenter.org/application/files/5616/8235/2328/Baker_Center_-_Mental_Health_and_Schools_Report_-_April_2023.pdf.
35. Darling-Hammond, Linda, and Channa Cook-Harvey. "Educating the Whole Child: Improving School Climate to Support Student Success." Learning Policy Institute, September 7, 2018. https://learningpolicyinstitute.org/product/educating-whole-child-report.
36. Darling-Hammond, Sean. "Fostering Belonging, Transforming Schools: The Impact of Restorative Practices." Learning Policy Institute, January 9, 2024. https://learningpolicyinstitute.org/product/impact-restorative-practices-report.
37. Darling-Hammond, Sean, Trevor Fronius, Hannah Sutherland, Sarah Guckenburg, Anthony Petrosino, and Nancy Hurley. "Effectiveness of Restorative Justice in US K-12 Schools: A Review of Quantitative Research (Webpage) – State Performance Plan Technical Assistance Project." Spptap.org, 2024. https://spptap.org/resources/effectiveness-of-restorative-justice-in-us-k-12-schools-a-review-of-quantitative-research-webpage/.
38. DePaoli, Jennifer, and Jennifer McCombs. "Keeping Students Safe: Policies and Practices That Work." Learning Policy Institute, January 26, 2024. https://learningpolicyinstitute.org/blog/transforming-schools-keeping-students-safe-policies-practices-work.
39. ———. "Safe Schools, Thriving Students: What We Know about Creating Safe and Supportive Schools." Learning Policy Institute, 2023. https://learningpolicyinstitute.org/product/safe-schools-thriving-students-brief.
40. DESSA. "How Can SEL Support Restorative Practices?" Aperture Education, November 13, 2023. https://apertureed.com/blog/can-sel-support-restorative-practices/.

41. DiNapoli, Thomas. "New York State School Safety: A Statewide and Regional Review," 2019. https://www.osc.ny.gov/files/local-government/publications/pdf/nys-school-safety-statewide-regional-review.pdf.
42. Divecha, Diana, and Marc Brackett. "Rethinking School-Based Bullying Prevention through the Lens of Social and Emotional Learning: A Bioecological Perspective." *International Journal of Bullying Prevention* 2, no. 2 (April 27, 2019): 93–113. https://doi.org/10.1007/s42380-019-00019-5.
43. Dorau, Bethany. "School Safety and Arming Teachers." www.ebsco.com. EBSCO, 2024. https://www.ebsco.com/research-starters/education/school-safety-and-arming-teachers-overview.
44. Duchesneau, Nancy. "Creating Safer Schools: A Case Study," 2023. /https://edtrust.org/wp-content/uploads/2014/09/Safer-Schools-V7.pdf.
45. Durisic, Masa, and Mila Bunijevac. "Parental Involvement as a Important Factor for Successful Education." *Parental Involvement as a Important Factor for Successful Education* 7, no. 3 (2017): 137–53. https://files.eric.ed.gov/fulltext/EJ1156936.pdf.
46. Encyclopaedia Britannica. "National Rifle Association of America | History & Facts." In *Encyclopædia Britannica*, 2019. https://www.britannica.com/topic/National-Rifle-Association-of-America.
47. Epstein, Joyce L. "Epstein's Framework of Six Types of Involvement (Including: Sample Practices, Challenges, Redefinitions, and Expected Results)," 2009. https://www.oregon.gov/ode/educator-resources/Documents/6typesj.epstien.pdf.
48. Evans, Molli, and Alissa Hebermehl. "Helping Students Feel Safe at School: 5 Essential Tips for School Staff." Caresolace.org, October 2024. https://www.caresolace.org/our-blog/helping-student-safety.
49. Evans, Robert. "Harlon Carter: The Man Who Militarized the Cops and the NRA (Multipart Series)," 2022. https://podcasts.apple.com/nz/podcast/part-one-harlon-carter-the-man-who-militarized-the/id1373812661?i=1000566354336.
50. Everytown for Gun Safety. "The Impact of Active Shooter Drills in Schools." Everytown Research & Policy, September 3, 2020. https://everytownresearch.org/report/the-impact-of-active-shooter-drills-in-schools/.
51. Eyrich, Tess. "Restorative Justice Shows Promise in K-12 Schools." Inside UCR, 2020. https://insideucr.ucr.edu/stories/2020/08/12/restorative-justice-shows-promise-k-12-schools.
52. Fallavollita, Westley. "Supporting Youth Loneliness & Social Isolation through Community-Based Mentoring | Youth-Nex Drive." Virginia.edu, 2021. https://youthnexdrive.virginia.edu/supporting-youth-loneliness-social-isolation-through-community-based-mentoring.
53. Freeman, Ie May, Jenny Tellez, and Anissa Jones. "Effectiveness of School Violence Prevention Programs in Elementary Schools in the United States: A Systematic Review." *Social Sciences* 13, no. 4 (April 1, 2024): 222. https://doi.org/10.3390/socsci13040222.
54. Garver, Rachel, and Pedro A Noguera. "For Safety's Sake: A Case Study of School Security Efforts and Their Impact on Education Reform." *The Journal of Applied Research on Children : Informing Policy for Children at Risk* 3, no. 2 (October 3, 2012). https://doi.org/10.58464/2155-5834.1090.
55. Gillham, Bobbi. *The Impact of Trauma-Informed School Practices on Positive Student Outcomes.* ProQuest LLC. ProQuest LLC. 789 East Eisenhower Parkway, P.O. Box 1346, Ann Arbor, MI 48106. Tel: 800-521-0600; Web site: http://www.proquest.com/en-

US/products/dissertations/individuals.shtml, 2023. https://eric.ed.gov/?q=trauma+informed+practices+outcome&id=ED634507.
56. Global Education Supplies and Solutions. "Ensuring Student Safety: The Importance of Safeguarding in Education | GESS Education." Gesseducation.com, February 6, 2024. https://www.gesseducation.com/gess-talks/articles/ensuring-student-safety-importance-safeguarding-education.
57. Goetschius, Leigh G., Vonnie C. McLoyd, Tyler C. Hein, Colter Mitchell, Luke W. Hyde, and Christopher S. Monk. "School Connectedness as a Protective Factor against Childhood Exposure to Violence and Social Deprivation: A Longitudinal Study of Adaptive and Maladaptive Outcomes." *Development and Psychopathology* 35, no. 3 (November 15, 2021): 1–16. https://doi.org/10.1017/s0954579421001140.
58. Goodman-Scott, Emily, Jennifer Betters-Bubon, Peg Donohue, and Jacob Olsen. *The School Counselor's Guide to Multi-Tiered Systems of Support*. Routledge, 2023.
59. Goodman-Scott, Emily, Jennifer Betters-Bubon, Jacob Olsen, and Peg Donohue. *Making MTSS Work*. American School Counselor Association, 2020.
60. Goodrich, Robert. "Opinion: Armed Guards and Surveillance Sacrifice True School Safety." CT Mirror, April 15, 2025. https://ctmirror.org/2025/04/15/armed-guards-and-surveillance-sacrifice-true-school-safety/.
61. Green, Emilee. "Exploring School Violence and Safety Concerns." icjia.illinois.gov, November 23, 2020. https://icjia.illinois.gov/researchhub/articles/exploring-school-violence-and-safety-concerns.
62. Gun Policy in America. "The Effects of Bans on the Sale of Assault Weapons and High-Capacity Magazines." Rand.org, July 16, 2024. https://www.rand.org/research/gun-policy/analysis/ban-assault-weapons.html.
63. Hammar Chiriac, Eva, Camilla Forsberg, and Robert Thornberg. "Teacher Teams: A Safe Place to Work on Creating and Maintaining a Positive School Climate." *Social Psychology of Education*, December 24, 2023. https://doi.org/10.1007/s11218-023-09880-1.
64. Harvard Catalyst. "Build a Mentoring Network." Harvard.edu, 2015. https://catalyst.harvard.edu/mentorship-in-clinical-and-translational-research/access-the-guide/build-a-mentoring-network/.
65. Hattersley, Robin. "Empowering Teachers to Survive and Protect during a School Crisis." Campus Safety Magazine, October 10, 2024. https://www.campussafetymagazine.com/insights/empowering-teachers-to-survive-and-protect-during-a-school-crisis/162361/.
66. Hedger, Joseph, and Celina Pierrottet. "California Ramps up Support for Community Schools." NASBE - National Association of State Boards of Education, 2025. https://www.nasbe.org/california-ramps-up-support-for-community-schools/.
67. Hirsch, Bomi. "Mentoring Programs to Prevent Youth Delinquency | County Health Rankings & Roadmaps." www.countyhealthrankings.org, December 13, 2023. https://www.countyhealthrankings.org/strategies-and-solutions/what-works-for-health/strategies/mentoring-programs-to-prevent-youth-delinquency.
68. Holland, Kristin M. "Characteristics of School-Associated Youth Homicides — United States, 1994–2018." *MMWR. Morbidity and Mortality Weekly Report* 68 (2019). https://doi.org/10.15585/mmwr.mm6803a1.
69. Hosokawa, Rikuya, Riho Tomozawa, and Megumi Fujimoto. "Effectiveness of Second Step Program in Fostering Social-Emotional Skills in Young Children: A Study in Japan." *BMC Pediatrics* 25, no. 1 (April 4, 2025). https://doi.org/10.1186/s12887-025-05624-6.

70. International Institute for Restorative Practices. "Restorative Practices and SEL Alignment," 2020. https://schoolguide.casel.org/uploads/sites/2/2020/12/2020.12.11_Aligning-SEL-and-RP_Final.pdf.
71. Jannetta, Jesse, Sam Tecotzky, Ashlin Oglesby-Neal, Maya White, J U S T I C E P O L I C Y C En, and T Er. "An Interim Process and Outcome Evaluation of Oakland's Measure Z-Funded Services," 2022. https://www.urban.org/sites/default/files/2024-12/Interim_Process_Evaluation_of_Oaklands_Measure_Z_Funded_Services_Department_of_Violence_Preventions_School_Violence_Intervention_and_Prevention_Strategy.pdf.
72. Jekielek, Susan, Kristin Moore, Elizabeth Hair, and Harriet Scarupa. "Mentoring: A Promising Strategy for Youth Development," 2002. https://cms.childtrends.org/wp-content/uploads/2002/02/MentoringRB.pdf.
73. Jennings, Chelsea. "Supportive Discipline." NASSP, December 1, 2021. https://www.nassp.org/publication/principal-leadership/volume-22-2021-2022/principal-leadership-december-2021/supportive-discipline/.
74. Jones Russell, Martha. "How Can Restorative Practices Decrease 'School to Prison Pipeline' Occurrences for Black Male Students? - Restorative Justice." Restorative Justice, 2015. https://restorativejustice.org/rj-archive/how-can-restorative-practices-decrease-school-to-prison-pipeline-occurrences-for-black-male-students/.
75. Jordan, Robert. "50-State School Safety Report." Sitesafetynet.org, 2025. https://sitesafetynet.org/50-state-school-safety-report/.
76. ———. "Parent Involvement in K-12 Education Safety." sitesafetynet.org, 2024. https://sitesafetynet.org/parent-involvement-in-k-12-education-safety/.
77. Jugl, Irina, Friedrich Lösel, Doris Bender, and Sonja King. "Psychosocial Prevention Programs against Radicalization and Extremism: A Meta-Analysis of Outcome Evaluations." *The European Journal of Psychology Applied to Legal Context* 13, no. 1 (December 2020): 37–46. https://doi.org/10.5093/ejpalc2021a6.
78. Justice Matters. "Restorative Practices in Schools." Justice Matters , 2019. https://www.justicemattersinkansas.org/restorative_practices_in_schools.
79. Kaufman, Michelle R., Kate Wright, Jeannette Simon, Giselle Edwards, Johannes Thrul, and David L. DuBois. "Mentoring in the Time of COVID-19: An Analysis of Online Focus Groups with Mentors to Youth." *American Journal of Community Psychology* 69, no. 1-2 (July 28, 2021). https://doi.org/10.1002/ajcp.12543.
80. Kearney, Christopher A., Ricardo Sanmartín, and Carolina Gonzálvez. "The School Climate and Academic Mindset Inventory (SCAMI): Confirmatory Factor Analysis and Invariance across Demographic Groups." *Frontiers in Psychology* 11 (August 14, 2020). https://doi.org/10.3389/fpsyg.2020.02061.
81. Kelly, Michael B, Anne B McBride, Jeff Bostic, and Sharon Hoover. "Chapter 11. Assessing and Addressing School Climate." *American Psychiatric Association Publishing EBooks*, July 11, 2019, 193–201. https://doi.org/10.1176/appi.books.9781615378845.lg11.
82. Kich, Martin. "How the NRA Has Devolved." Academe Blog, March 19, 2018. https://academeblog.org/2018/03/19/how-the-nra-has-devolved/.
83. King-White, Dakota. "Five Strategies to Develop Mental Health Models in Schools." www.counseling.org. American Counseling Association, 2018. https://www.counseling.org/resources/topics/professional-counseling/school-based-professional-counselors/legacy/five-strategies-to-develop-mental-health-models-in-schools.

84. Klarevas, Louis. "Letter to the Editor Re: DiMaggio, C. Et Al. "Changes in U.S. Mass Shooting Deaths Associated with the 1994-2004 Federal Assault Weapons Ban." *Journal of Trauma and Acute Care Surgery* 86, no. 5 (February 2019): 1. https://doi.org/10.1097/01586154-900000000-98411.
85. ———. *Rampage Nation : Securing America from Mass Shootings*. Amherst, New York: Prometheus Books, 2016.
86. Klarevas, Louis, Andrew Conner, and David Hemenway. "The Effect of Large-Capacity Magazine Bans on High-Fatality Mass Shootings, 1990–2017." *American Journal of Public Health* 109, no. 12 (December 2019): 1754–61. https://doi.org/10.2105/ajph.2019.305411.
87. Lafortune, Julien, Laura Hill, Niu Gao, Joseph Herrera, Emmanuel Prutny, Darriya Starr, Bruce Fuller, Julian Betts, Karna Malaviya, and Jonathan Isler. "District Spending of One-Time Funds for Educational Recovery." Public Policy Institute of California, June 28, 2023. https://www.ppic.org/publication/district-spending-of-one-time-funds-for-educational-recovery/.
88. Larson, Jim. "Best Practices in School Violence Prevention," n.d. https://apps.nasponline.org/resources-and-publications/books-and-products/products/books/docs/bp6/book_3_w/16_B3chapter16_WM.pdf.
89. Learning Policy Institute. "School Safety, Discipline, and Restorative Practices." Learning Policy Institute, May 20, 2024. https://learningpolicyinstitute.org/topic/school-safety-discipline-and-restorative-practices.
90. Lefkowitz-Rao, Isabella . "Examining the Impact of School Resource Officers and Possible Alternatives." Juvjustice.org, 2024. https://www.juvjustice.org/blog/1491.
91. Lim, Jin Hyung, Ella Rho, and Chunyan Yang. "Evidence-Based Practices of Culturally Responsive Social and Emotional Learning (SEL) Programs: A Systematic Review and Meta-Analysis." *School Psychology Review*, November 26, 2024, 1–16. https://doi.org/10.1080/2372966x.2024.2432853.
92. Lindstrom Johnson, Sarah, Andrea N. Montes, Brooke Johnson, and Anthony Peguero. "School Safety Program Evaluation School Year 2020-2021." Arizona State University, 2021. https://www.azed.gov/sites/default/files/2021/12/SSP%20Evaluation%20FY21.pdf.
93. Lodi, Ernesto, Lucrezia Perrella, Gian Luigi Lepri, Maria Luisa Scarpa, and Patrizia Patrizi. "Use of Restorative Justice and Restorative Practices at School: A Systematic Literature Review." *International Journal of Environmental Research and Public Health* 19, no. 1 (2021): 96. https://doi.org/10.3390/ijerph19010096.
94. Louisiana Department of Education. "Social-Emotional Learning Curricula and Strategies Portfolio 1 a Portfolio of Evidence-Based Social-Emotional Learning (SEL) Curricula and Strategies for Louisiana," 2019. https://www.hsredesign.org/wp-content/uploads/2019/10/social-emotional-learning-sel-curricula-and-strategies-portfolio.pdf.
95. Mahoney, Joseph, Joseph Durlak, and Roger Weissberg. "An Update on Social and Emotional Learning Outcome Research - Kappanonline.org." kappanonline.org, November 26, 2018. https://kappanonline.org/social-emotional-learning-outcome-research-mahoney-durlak-weissberg/.
96. Making Waves Education Foundation. "Networking and Mentorship - Making Waves Education Foundation." Making Waves Education Foundation, December 23, 2024. https://making-waves.org/career/networking-and-mentorship/.

97. Marraccini, Marisa E., and Zoe M. F. Brier. "School Connectedness and Suicidal Thoughts and Behaviors: A Systematic Meta-Analysis." *School Psychology Quarterly* 32, no. 1 (March 2017): 5–21. https://doi.org/10.1037/spq0000192.
98. Martin, Alexis. "Advancing School-Based Mental Health in California." *Childrenspartnership.org*, 2022. https://childrenspartnership.org/wp-content/uploads/2022/02/TCP-Brief_Advancing-School-Based-Mental-Health-Centers.pdf.
99. Martin, Cody. "Communication Methods for School Safety: Best Practices and Strategies." Risk Strategy Group, June 12, 2023. https://riskstrategygroup.com/communication-methods-for-school-safety-best-practices-and-strategies/.
100. Martins Caridade, Sónia Maria, Hélder Fernando Pedrosa e Sousa, and Maria Alzira Pimenta Dinis. "The Mediating Effect of Parental Involvement on School Climate and Behavior Problems: School Personnel Perceptions." *Behavioral Sciences* 10, no. 8 (August 9, 2020): 129. https://doi.org/10.3390/bs10080129.
101. Massachusetts Teachers Association. "Safe Schools for All Task Force." Mass Teacher Association, 2025. https://massteacher.org/about-the-mta/committees/safe-schools-for-all-task-force.
102. McCullom, Rod. "Are Schools with Armed Police Actually Safer?" Undark Magazine, November 6, 2024. https://undark.org/2024/11/06/are-schools-with-armed-police-actually-safer/.
103. Mcmorris, Barbara, Kara Beckman, Glynis Ma, Jenna Shea, Rachel Baumgartner, and Eggert. "Applying Restorative Practices to Minneapolis Public Schools Students Recommended for Possible Expulsion a Pilot Program Evaluation of the Family and Youth Restorative Conference Program Final Report -December 2013 School of Nursing Healthy Youth Development • Prevention Research Center," 2013. https://chyd.umn.edu/sites/hyd.umn.edu/files/2024-01/Beckman_LRC.pdf.
104. Mental Health America. "Discipline and Positive Behavior Support in Schools | Mental Health America." Mental Health America, February 24, 2025. https://mhanational.org/position-statements/discipline-and-positive-behavior-support-in-schools/.
105. Mental Health Services Oversight and Accountability Commission. "Schools as Centers of Wellness," 2020. https://bhsoac.ca.gov/wp-content/uploads/schools_as_centers_of_wellness_final-2.pdf.
106. MENTOR. "Starting a Youth Mentoring Program: 9 Maintaining the Program - MENTOR." MENTOR.org, November 16, 2020. https://www.mentoring.org/resource/maintaining-the-program/.
107. Mowen, Thomas J. "Parental Involvement in School and the Role of School Security Measures." *Education and Urban Society* 47, no. 7 (November 7, 2013): 830–48. https://doi.org/10.1177/0013124513508581.
108. Naftzger, Neil, and Dominique Bradley. "Chicago Public Schools Community Schools Initiative | American Institutes for Research." American Institutes for Research, 2022. https://www.air.org/project/chicago-public-schools-community-schools-initiative.
109. Napolitan, Larissa. "How Duneland Increased Consistency and Communication for Student Interventions." Branchingminds.com. Branching Minds, September 24, 2024. https://www.branchingminds.com/success-stories/how-duneland-increased-consistency-and-communication-for-student-interventions.
110. NASP. "Comprehensive School-Based Mental and Behavioral Health Services and School Psychologists." National Association of School Psychologists (NASP), 2021.

https://www.nasponline.org/resources-and-publications/resources-and-podcasts/mental-and-behavioral-health/additional-resources/comprehensive-school-based-mental-and-behavioral-health-services-and-school-psychologists.
111. National Association of School Psychologists. "Effective School-Community Partnerships to Support School Mental Health," n.d. https://www.schoolmentalhealth.org/media/som/microsites/ncsmh/documents/fliers-resources-misc-docs/resources/Effective-School-Comm-Partnerships-to-support-SMH-Final.pdf.
112. ———. "School Violence Prevention." National Association of School Psychologists (NASP), 2015. https://www.nasponline.org/resources-and-publications/resources-and-podcasts/school-safety-and-crisis/school-violence-resources/school-violence-prevention.
113. ———. "School Violence Prevention: Tips for Parents & Educators." National Association of School Psychologists (NASP), n.d. https://www.nasponline.org/resources-and-publications/resources-and-podcasts/school-safety-and-crisis/school-violence-resources/school-violence-prevention/school-violence-prevention-tips-for-parents-and-educators.
114. National Center for Education Statistics. "Press Release - New Schools Data Examine Violent Incidents, Bullying, Drug Possession, 'Restorative' Practices, Security Staff, and More - January 17, 2024." nces.ed.gov. National Center for Education Statistics, January 17, 2024. https://nces.ed.gov/whatsnew/press_releases/1_17_2024.asp.
115. National Center for School Mental Health. "School Mental Health Quality Guide: Funding and Sustainability." NCSMH, University of Maryland School of Medicine, 2023. https://www.schoolmentalhealth.org/media/som/microsites/ncsmh/documents/quality-guides/Funding-&-Sustainability.pdf.
116. National Center on Safe Supportive Learning Environments. "Implementing School Mental Health Supports: Best Practices in Action." US Department of Education, n.d. https://safesupportivelearning.ed.gov/sites/default/files/13-ImpSchMnHlthSprtBtPrt-508_0.pdf.
117. ———. "School Climate Improvement." safesupportivelearning.ed.gov, 2023. https://safesupportivelearning.ed.gov/school-climate-improvement.
118. National Education Association. "National Education Association Policy Statements," 2022. https://www.nea.org/sites/default/files/2024-01/nea-policy-on-safe-just-and-equitable-schools-2022.pdf.
119. National Institute of Justice. "The Comprehensive School Safety Initiative: Awards Made in Fiscal Year 2015." US Department of Justice, 2016. https://www.ojp.gov/pdffiles1/nij/249228.pdf.
120. National Mentoring Resource Center. "Saving Lives & Inspiring Youth (S.L.I.Y): A Cross-Age Peer Mentoring Program - National Mentoring Resource Center." National Mentoring Resource Center, November 9, 2016. https://nationalmentoringresourcecenter.org/blog/saving-lives-inspiring-youth-s-l-i-y-a-cross-age-peer-mentoring-program/.
121. National Rifle Association. "About the NRA." Nra.org. National Rifle Association, 2024. https://home.nra.org/about-the-nra/.
122. ———. "An NRA Shooting Sports Journal | NRA: Early Foundation and Development 1871-1907." An NRA Shooting Sports Journal, 2020. https://www.ssusa.org/content/nra-early-foundation-and-development-1871-1907/.

123. ———. "Cincinnati '77: Birthplace of the Modern NRA." National Rifle Association, 2019. https://www.americanrifleman.org/content/cincinnati-77-birthplace-of-the-modern-nra/.
124. National School Climate Center. "Practical Strategies for Building a Positive School Climate - National School Climate Center." National School Climate Center, August 23, 2024. https://schoolclimate.org/practical-strategies-for-building-a-positive-school-climate/.
125. New Jersey Department of Education. "Social and Emotional Learning." www.nj.gov, n.d. https://www.nj.gov/education/safety/wellness/selearning/.
126. Newtown Public Schools. "Safe School Climate Policy." newtown-policies.campuscontact.com, 2017. https://newtown-policies.campuscontact.com/5131.914-SafeSchoolClimatePolicy.
127. Nickerson, Amanda. "Can SEL Reduce School Violence?" ASCD, 2018. https://www.ascd.org/el/articles/can-sel-reduce-school-violence.
128. O'connor, Ann, Jenna Strawhun, Natalie Hoff, and Reece Petersen. "Resources: Social Skills Curricula & Programs," 2014. https://nemtss.unl.edu/wp-content/uploads/2024/12/Resources-for-Social-Skills-Curricula-9-22-14.pdf.
129. O'Malley, Meagan, and Angela Amarillas. "What Works Brief #4: School Connectedness." WestEd, 2025. https://www.wested.org/resource/what-works-brief-4-school-connectedness/.
130. Ohio Department of Education. "Ohio's Comprehensive School Safety Framework: A Guide to Support Local Implementation," 2023. https://dam.assets.ohio.gov/image/upload/ohioschoolsafetycenter.ohio.gov/2023-School-Safety-Comprehensive-Guide.pdf.
131. ———. "School-Based Mental Health." Ohio.gov, 2023. https://education.ohio.gov/Topics/Student-Supports/School-Wellness/School-based-Mental-Health.
132. Panchal, Nirmita, Cynthia Cox, and Robin Rudowitz. "The Landscape of School-Based Mental Health Services." KFF, September 6, 2022. https://www.kff.org/mental-health/issue-brief/the-landscape-of-school-based-mental-health-services/.
133. Pas, Elise. "Leveraging Restorative Practices and Social Emotional Learning to Enhance Transitioning and Early High School Students' Engagement | IES." Ed.gov, 2020. https://ies.ed.gov/use-work/awards/leveraging-restorative-practices-and-social-emotional-learning-enhance-transitioning-and-early-high.
134. Patchin, Justin W. "Developing a Positive School Climate to Prevent Bullying and Cyberbullying." Cyberbullying Research Center, February 17, 2019. https://cyberbullying.org/developing-a-positive-school-climate-to-prevent-bullying-and-cyberbullying.
135. Pattengill, Derby. "Supporting a Positive School Climate," 2024. https://www.csba.org/-/media/CSBA/Files/GovernanceResources/SafeSchoolsToolkit/Safety-Toolkit-4.ashx?la=en&rev=1754646702b04b4285aef8d60dd281dc.
136. Peterson, Reece L., and Russell Skiba. "Creating School Climates That Prevent School Violence." *Preventing School Failure: Alternative Education for Children and Youth* 44, no. 3 (January 2000): 122–29. https://doi.org/10.1080/10459880009599794.
137. promiseneighborhoods.ed.gov. "Promise Neighborhoods," n.d. https://promiseneighborhoods.ed.gov/.
138. PTA.org. "Blueprint for Working with State Legislators to Improve School Safety | National PTA." Pta.org, 2024. https://www.pta.org/home/family-

resources/safety/School-Safety/blueprint-for-working-with-state-legislators-to-improve-school-safety.
139. Public Safety Canada. "National Strategy on Countering Radicalization to Violence." www.publicsafety.gc.ca, December 21, 2018. https://www.publicsafety.gc.ca/cnt/rsrcs/pblctns/ntnl-strtg-cntrng-rdclztn-vlnc/index-en.aspx.
140. Purbasari, Anisa. "Drive Employee Skill Development with Mentoring." Chronus, March 24, 2023. https://chronus.com/blog/drive-employee-skill-development.
141. Ramya Ramadurai. "Addressing Loneliness in Youth: Review Underscores Effective Intervention Strategies – the Chronicle of Evidence-Based Mentoring." Evidencebasedmentoring.org, January 25, 2025. https://www.evidencebasedmentoring.org/addressing-loneliness-in-youth-review-underscores-effective-intervention-strategies/.
142. Readiness and Emergency Management for Schools. "School Climate and Emergencies." rems.ed.gov, n.d. https://rems.ed.gov/K12SchoolClimateandEmerg.aspx.
143. Rennie, Peggy. "For Children and Youth Who Are, or Have Been in Receipt of Child Protective Services," 2016. https://peelyork.bigbrothersbigsisters.ca/wp-content/uploads/sites/160/2017/10/Min_of_Youth_AT_A_GLANCE_v0.2.pdf.
144. Reynolds, Heather. "Reimagining School Safety." American Federation of Teachers, March 21, 2023. https://www.aft.org/ae/spring2023/reynolds_astor.
145. Richards, Annie. "A Holistic Approach to Enhancing School Safety: 5 Essential Steps and Strategies." Vector Solutions, 2024. https://www.vectorsolutions.com/resources/blogs/a-holistic-approach-to-enhancing-school-safety/.
146. Riedman, David. "K-12 School Shooting Database." K-12 School Shooting Database, 2023. https://k12ssdb.org/.
147. Rivera, Autumn. "Supporting Safe Schools: A Report Focused on Prevention, Response, and Positive Climate." Ncsl.org, 2025. https://www.ncsl.org/education/supporting-safe-schools-a-report-focused-on-prevention-response-and-positive-climate.
148. Rose, Chad. "Evaluation of the K-5 Second Step Social-Emotional Learning Program and Bully Prevention Unit: Impact on Youth Violence and School Climate among Students with and at Risk for Disability Identification | IES." Ed.gov, 2024. https://ies.ed.gov/use-work/awards/evaluation-k-5-second-step-social-emotional-learning-program-and-bully-prevention-unit-impact-youth.
149. Rothman, Lily. "The Original Reason the NRA Was Founded." Time. Time, November 17, 2015. https://time.com/4106381/nra-1871-history/.
150. Safe and Sound Schools. "Parents for Safer Schools: A School-Based Volunteer Program for Parents and Caregivers," 2019. https://www.safeandsoundschools.org/_files/ugd/d12b1c_b084e1541ae942cba0bc84af8bdce13a.pdf.
151. Safe Supportive Learning. "Preventing Violence and Building Safe School Communities: A Guide for Creating Student-Led Clubs." safesupportivelearning.ed.gov, 2024. https://safesupportivelearning.ed.gov/sites/default/files/2025-01/NCSSLE-CVl-StdntSftyGde-508.pdf.
152. Sandy Hook Promise. "Sandy Hook Promise Statement on the Reintroduction of the PLAN for School Safety Act." Sandy Hook Promise, April 2, 2025. https://www.sandyhookpromise.org/press-releases/statement-on-the-reintroduction-of-the-plan-for-school-safety-act/.

153. Saucedo, Erik. "California's Community Schools Initiative: Progress and Impact." California Budget and Policy Center, 2024. https://calbudgetcenter.org/resources/californias-community-schools-initiative-progress-and-impact/.
154. School Safety. "Foundational Elements of School Safety | SchoolSafety.gov." www.schoolsafety.gov, n.d. https://www.schoolsafety.gov/foundational-elements-school-safety.
155. "School-Based Mental Health: An Empirical Guide for Decision-Makers | 67." Accessed May 16, 2025. http://rtckids.fmhi.usf.edu/rtcpubs/study04/SBMHchapter6.pdf.
156. SchoolHouse Connection. "Policies and Practices to Address School Discipline and Student Homelessness." SchoolHouse Connection, February 20, 2025. https://schoolhouseconnection.org/article/policies-and-practices-to-address-school-discipline-and-student-homelessness.
157. SchoolSafety.gov. "Mental Health Resources," n.d. https://www.schoolsafety.gov/sites/default/files/2023-05/Mental%20Health%20Resources.pdf.
158. Schreiber, Allison, Brent Miller, and Kiera Dressler. "An Introduction to Restorative Practices," 2022. https://www.nc2s.org/wp-content/uploads/2022/07/An-Introduction-to-Restorative-Practices.pdf.
159. Sigrist, Gary. "Building Safe Learning Environments: The Role of Mental Health in School Safety | Safeguard Risk Solutions, LLC." Safeguard Risk Solutions, LLC, 2024. https://safeguardrisksolutions.com/building-safe-learning-environments-the-role-of-mental-health-in-school-safety/.
160. Soma, Caelan. "Protecting Schools from Violence: What Matters Most? | Michigan Association of Superintendents & Administrators." Michigan Association of Superintendents & Administrators, June 3, 2024. https://gomasa.org/2024/06/03/protecting-schools-from-violence-what-matters-most/.
161. Song, Wei, Xueqin Qian, and Bradley Goodnight. "Examining the Roles of Parents and Community Involvement and Prevention Programs in Reducing School Violence." *Journal of School Violence* 18, no. 3 (2019): 403–20. https://eric.ed.gov/?id=EJ1214619.
162. Stepansky, Joseph. "US Lawmakers Banned Assault Weapons in 1994. Why Can't They Now?" www.aljazeera.com, April 20, 2023. https://www.aljazeera.com/news/2023/4/20/us-legislators-banned-assault-weapons-in-94-why-cant-they-now.
163. Stilwell, Sarah, Briana Scott, Esther Lee, Heather Murphy, Erin Wyatt, Carolyn Seiger, and Brent Miller. "Cultivating a Supportive School Climate: A 'How To' Guide," 2024. https://www.nc2s.org/wp-content/uploads/2024/09/Cultivating-a-Supportive-School-Climate-A-22How-To22-Guide.pdf.
164. Stockdale, Sadie. "UChicago Education Lab Study Finds Decrease in Arrests, Suspensions in Schools That Use Restorative Practices." University of Chicago News, September 21, 2023. https://news.uchicago.edu/story/uchicago-education-lab-study-finds-decrease-arrests-suspensions-schools-use-restorative.
165. Substance Abuse and Mental Health Services Administration. "Examining the Use of Braided Funding for Substance Use Disorder Services Examining the Use of Braided Funding for Substance Use Disorder Services I Acknowledgement," 2024. https://library.samhsa.gov/sites/default/files/cfri-braided-funding-report-pep23-06-07-002.pdf.

166. The Up Center. "The Power of Mentorship: Why Every Child Needs a Positive Role Model." The Up Center, March 21, 2025. https://theupcenter.org/power-of-mentorship-why-every-child-needs-role-model/.
167. The White House. "The Cumulative Costs of Gun Violence on Students and Schools | CEA | the White House." The White House, January 15, 2025. https://bidenwhitehouse.archives.gov/cea/written-materials/2025/01/15/the-cumulative-costs-of-gun-violence-on-students-and-schools/.
168. Thomas, Selin. "How the NRA Forged Its Scorched-Earth Strategy." The Trace, April 23, 2024. https://www.thetrace.org/2024/04/nra-politics-influence-lobbying-history/.
169. Travis, David. "Impacts of the 1994 Assault Weapons Ban: 1994–96." *Displays* 20, no. 4 (December 1999): 163. https://doi.org/10.1016/s0141-9382(99)00018-9.
170. Trump, Kenneth. "Best Practices for School Security and Emergency Preparedness Planning." National School Safety and Security Services, n.d. https://schoolsecurity.org/trends/best-practices-for-school-security-and-emergency-preparedness-planning/.
171. ———. "Parents and School Safety." National School Safety and Security Services, n.d. https://schoolsecurity.org/resource/parents-and-school-safety/.
172. Trust for America's Health. "Braiding and Blending Funds to Support Community Health Improvement: A Compendium of Resources and Examples," 2018. https://www.tfah.org/wp-content/uploads/2018/01/TFAH-Braiding-Blending-Compendium-FINAL.pdf.
173. UNESCO. "What You Need to Know about Ending Violence in and through Education." Unesco.org, 2024. https://www.unesco.org/en/articles/what-you-need-know-about-ending-violence-and-through-education.
174. University of Illinois Chicago. "New Study Finds Mentorship Lowers Rates of Youth Crime and Delinquency | School of Public Health | University of Illinois Chicago." School of Public Health, October 17, 2022. https://publichealth.uic.edu/news-stories/new-study-finds-mentorship-lowers-rates-of-youth-crime-and-delinquency/.
175. University of Southampton. "The Benefits of a Mentoring Relationship." Southampton.ac.uk, 2012. https://www.southampton.ac.uk/professional-development/mentoring/benefits-of-a-mentoring-relationship.page.
176. US Department of Education. "Guiding Principles for Creating Safe, Inclusive, Supportive, and Fair School Climates," March 2023. https://www.ed.gov/sites/ed/files/policy/gen/guid/school-discipline/guiding-principles.pdf.
177. Virginia Department of Criminal Justice Services. "Mental Health and Trauma Support | Virginia Department of Criminal Justice Services." Virginia.gov, 2025. https://www.cms.dcjs.virginia.gov/virginia-center-school-and-campus-safety/mental-health-and-trauma-support.
178. Waldman, Michael. "How the NRA Rewrote the Second Amendment." www.brennancenter.org. The Brennan Center for Justice, May 20, 2014. https://www.brennancenter.org/our-work/research-reports/how-nra-rewrote-second-amendment.
179. Walker, Tim. "Do Restorative Practices Work? | NEA." www.nea.org, November 8, 2023. https://www.nea.org/nea-today/all-news-articles/do-restorative-practices-work.
180. Wallner, Claudia. "The Contested Relationship between Youth and Violent Extremism Assessing the Evidence Base in Relation to P/CVE Interventions," 2021. https://connect.unoct-connectandlearn.org/system/files/2024-

12/RUSI%20The%20Contested%20Relationship%20Between%20Youth%20234_op_pcve_youth_web_version_0.pdf.
181. Washington Office of Superintendent of Public Instruction. "Social Emotional Learning Professional Development Menu 2024-2025 SEL Professional Learning Requirement," 2024. https://ospi.k12.wa.us/sites/default/files/2024-08/guidance_selprofessionaldevelopmentmenu24-25.pdf.
182. Wellable. "Teacher Well-Being: 8 Ways to Support the Superheroes of Education." Wellable, August 1, 2023. https://www.wellable.co/blog/teacher-well-being-8-ways-to-support-the-superheroes-of-education/.
183. Werntz, Alexandra, Jean E. Rhodes, Hannah Brockstein, Lindsay Fallon, and Amy Cook. "A Scoping Review of Therapeutic Mentoring for Youth Mental Health." *Frontiers in Child and Adolescent Psychiatry* 4 (January 27, 2025). https://doi.org/10.3389/frcha.2025.1509971.
184. West Linn-Wilsonville School District. "Positive School Communities and Restorative Practices." K12.or.us, 2024. https://www.wlwv.k12.or.us/Page/15150.
185. Whalen, Christina. "Preventing School Violence: Building a Safer Future." RethinkEd. Rethink Ed, March 2, 2023. http://rethinked.com/resources/preventing-school-violence-building-a-safer-future/.
186. Williams, Matigan. "The Failed Promise of Gun Legislation: The Assault Weapons Ban the Failed Promise of Gun Legislation: The Assault Weapons Ban and Sandy Hook and Sandy Hook," 2024. https://scholarship.depauw.edu/cgi/viewcontent.cgi?article=1236&context=studentresearch.
187. Winterbotham, Emily. "How Effective Are Mentorship Interventions? Assessing the Evidence Base for Preventing and Countering Violent Extremism," 2020. https://static.rusi.org/pcve_mentorship_final_web_version.pdf.
188. Woolf, Nick. "6 Strategies to Increase Parent Engagement in SEL | Panorama Education." www.panoramaed.com, n.d. https://www.panoramaed.com/blog/6-strategies-parent-engagement-social-emotional-learning.
189. Yusem, David, Denise Curtis, Komoia Johnson, and Barbara McClung. "Oakland Unified School District Restorative Justice Implementation Guide." *Seattle Public Schools*, 2023. https://www.seattleschools.org/wp-content/uploads/2023/02/OUSD-Implementation-Guide.pdf.

www.ingramcontent.com/pod-product-compliance
Lightning Source LLC
Chambersburg PA
CBHW020534030426
42337CB00013B/849